CECIL COUNTY
PUBLIC LIBRARY
JUL 0 9 2009   301 Newark Ave.
Elkton, MD 21921

O9-BHJ-199

Wanda E. Brunstetter's

Amish
Friends
COOKBOOK
VOLUME 2

Wanda E. Brunstetter's

Amish
Friends
COOKBOOK
VOLUME 2

200 Hearty Recipes from Amish Country

BARBOUR
PUBLISHING

© 2009 by Wanda E. Brunstetter

ISBN 978-1-60260-345-5

All rights reserved. No part of this publication may be reproduced or transmitted for commercial purposes, except for brief quotations in printed reviews, without written permission of the publisher.

Churches and other noncommercial interests may reproduce portions of this book without the express written permission of Barbour Publishing, provided that the text does not exceed 500 words and that the text is not material quoted from another publisher. When reproducing text from this book, include the following credit line: "From *Wanda E. Brunstetter's Amish Friends Cookbook, Volume 2*, published by Barbour Publishing, Inc. Used by permission."

All scripture quotations are taken from the King James Version of the Bible.

Cover image © Doyle Yoder

Published by Barbour Publishing, Inc., P.O. Box 719, Uhrichsville, Ohio 44683, www.barbourbooks.com

Our mission is to publish and distribute inspirational products offering exceptional value and biblical encouragement to the masses.

 Member of the
Evangelical Christian
Publishers Association

Printed in China.

Dedication

To my Amish friends in various parts of America.
Thank you for sharing your recipes with me.

Contents

Amish across America

In the 1700s, after much persecution for their Anabaptist religious beliefs, the Amish, along with the Mennonites, left their homes in Germany and Switzerland and immigrated to North America, arriving in eastern Pennsylvania. As Amish communities continued to grow and seek more land, new Amish communities were started in other areas. Today there are Amish communities in many parts of the United States and Canada, and new ones continue to appear. The Amish population has grown to over two hundred thousand nationwide.

While all Amish adhere to the regulation of their Ordnung (church rules), many communities differ in practice, appearance, style of their homes, and types of buggies.

Throughout this cookbook you will find information about several Amish communities of which I have personal knowledge. I hope it will help you understand the Amish people a little better as you learn some of the varying differences between communities.

Beverages

And also that every man should eat and drink,
and enjoy the good of all his labour, it is the gift of God.

ECCLESIASTES 3:13

Icy Holiday Punch

1 (6 ounce) package orange gelatin (or 6 tablespoons)

¾ cup sugar

2 cups boiling water

1 (46 ounce) can pineapple juice

6 cups cold water

2 liters ginger ale

1 (1 quart container) orange sherbet

In 4-quart freezer-proof container, dissolve gelatin and sugar in boiling water. Stir in pineapple juice and cold water. Cover and freeze overnight. Remove from freezer 2 hours before serving. Place in punch bowl. Stir in ginger ale and orange sherbet just before serving. Yield: 32 to 36 servings (6 quarts)

Wilma Yoder
Dundee, Ohio

Lemon Shake-Up

2 cups sugar

1 cup water

1 cup fresh lemon juice

Boil sugar and water 5 minutes. Cool and add lemon juice. Store in refrigerator. Add 2 tablespoons to 8-ounce glass of water with ice. Very refreshing!

Betty Miller
Goshen, Indiana

> *Anyone who has*
> *a heart full of friend-*
> *ship has a hard time*
> *finding enemies.*

Amish Wine

1 (16 ounce) can frozen orange juice concentrate
1 (16 ounce) can frozen grape juice concentrate
1 cup sugar
¼ cup lemon juice
1 (2 liter) bottle Sprite

Mix ingredients and add ice.

Dianna Yoder
Goshen, Indiana

Rhubarb Drink

1½ cups sugar
3 cups rhubarb, cut in pieces
4 cups water
Juice of one lemon
¼ cup frozen orange juice concentrate
1 liter ginger ale
Water to taste

Cook sugar, rhubarb, and 4 cups water 5 minutes. Add lemon juice and orange juice concentrate. Put mixture through a strainer. Freeze or can. Mix with ginger ale and add water to taste.

Miriam Blank
Narvon, Pennsylvania

Russian Tea

1¾ cups Tang
½ cup Nestea
⅓ cup sugar
1 cup lemonade mix
1 teaspoon cinnamon

Mix well and store in airtight container. Stir 2 teaspoons of mix into 1 cup hot water.

Mrs. David Graber
Bloomfield, Iowa

An investment in knowledge always pays the best interest.

Homemade Hot Chocolate

9 cups nonfat dry powdered milk
1 (16 ounce) box chocolate drink mix (3¼ cups)
    or Nesquik powder
1 (6 ounce) can dry coffee creamer
2 cups powdered sugar

Mix well and store in airtight container. Stir ¼ cup mix into 1 cup hot water.

Mrs. Jerry J. Miller
Spartanburg, Pennsylvania

*May the
hinges of friendship
never grow rusty.*

Fruit Punch

1 (12 to 16 ounce) can frozen orange juice concentrate
1 (6 ounce) can frozen lemonade concentrate
1 (6 ounce) can frozen pineapple juice concentrate
3 cups water
1 pint orange sherbet
1 quart ginger ale
1 tray ice cubes

Place concentrates in punch bowl. Add water and stir. Add sherbet. Pour ginger ale over sherbet and add ice cubes. Stir and serve.

Linda Fisher
Leola, Pennsylvania

Red Ribbon Punch

1 (46 ounce) can red Hawaiian Punch
1 (6 ounce) can frozen pineapple juice
1 (28 ounce) bottle chilled 7-UP
2 (16 ounce) bottles orange-pineapple soda (or orange soda)
1 quart pineapple sherbet

Mix ingredients in large container. Double recipe to make punch bowl full. Freeze some punch in two ring molds to use in punch bowl while serving.

Joanna Miller
Hersey, Michigan

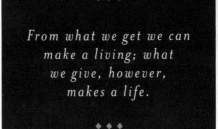

♦ ♦ ♦

From what we get we can make a living; what we give, however, makes a life.

♦ ♦ ♦

Orange Peach Smoothies

2 cups frozen peach slices, unthawed

I cup milk

I (6 ounce) can frozen orange juice concentrate, thawed

¼ teaspoon almond extract

I pint vanilla ice cream

In blender combine peaches, milk, orange juice concentrate, and extract. Add ice cream. Cover and process until smooth. Pour into glasses; serve immediately. Yield: 4 servings

Elva Shirk
Dundee, New York

Egg Nog Drink

2 eggs

I cup sugar

¼ teaspoon salt

¼ teaspoon nutmeg

2 quarts cold milk

½ teaspoon vanilla

Beat eggs well. Beat in sugar, salt, and nutmeg. Stir into milk until sugar is dissolved. Add vanilla. Chill and serve.

Mary Yoder
Waldron, Michigan

Wedding Punch

1 package cherry Kool-Aid
1 package strawberry Kool-Aid
2 quarts plus 2 cups water
2 cups sugar
1 (46 ounce) can orange juice
1 (46 ounce) can pineapple juice
2 quarts ginger ale
Ice

Combine all ingredients and stir until Kool-Aid and sugar are dissolved. Serve with ice.

Laura Byler
Woodhull, New York

Tea Concentrate

1 quart water
1 cup sugar
2 cups tea leaves, packed

Bring water and sugar to a boil. Remove from heat. Add tea leaves, cover, and let steep 5 to 7 minutes. Strain mixture and add water and ice to make one gallon. Concentrate may be frozen.

Karen Lehman
Bristol, Indiana

Lancaster County, Pennsylvania

Lancaster County, Pennsylvania, has the second highest population of Amish. The Amish in Lancaster County drive gray, box-shaped buggies, which sets them apart from many other Amish communities where black buggies are driven.

The farmland in Lancaster County is very productive, with rich soil good for growing a variety of crops. Many of the Amish in this area used to rely solely on farming as their primary income, but due to high prices and lack of land, a lot of Amish men now work at other jobs to support their families. Some have home-based businesses, while others work outside the home at local places of business.

Lancaster County is a popular tourist destination because there is so much to see and do in the area. The many farmer's markets in or near Lancaster County bring in people from far and wide.

Local volunteer fire companies in Lancaster County raise funds through what they call "mud sales." Many of the items available at these auction events are sold outside during the spring when the weather is wet and the ground becomes muddy. Hence, the name "mud sales." Auctioned items often include furniture, tools, quilts, building materials, livestock, Amish buggies, farming equipment, and garden items.

Today there are more than twenty-five different Amish, Mennonite, and Brethren church groups in Lancaster County. The more traditional groups do not permit electricity or telephones in their homes, but they make use of phone sheds. Some, who have businesses, make use of cell phones.

Separation from the rest of society and its worldly ways helps strengthen the Amish community.

Breads and Rolls

Give her of the fruit of her hands;
and let her own works praise her in the gates.

PROVERBS 31:31

Applesauce Spice Puffs

2 cups dry baking mix
⅓ cup sugar
1 teaspoon cinnamon
¼ teaspoon cloves
¼ teaspoon nutmeg
½ cup applesauce
¼ cup milk
1 egg, beaten
2 tablespoons vegetable oil

Topping:
½ cup butter, melted
1 teaspoon cinnamon
½ cup white sugar

Preheat oven to 400 degrees. Sift baking mix and stir in sugar and spices. Add applesauce, milk, egg, and oil. Fill greased muffin tins two-thirds full. Bake 12 minutes. Brush tops with melted butter and dip in cinnamon sugar mixture. Serve warm.

Irene Miller
Shipshewana, Indiana

Iced Cinnamon Biscuits

2 cups flour
¼ cup sugar
1 tablespoon baking powder
1 teaspoon salt
1 teaspoon cinnamon
¼ teaspoon soda
⅓ cup shortening
½ cup raisins
¾ cup buttermilk

Preheat oven to 450 degrees. Combine first six ingredients. Cut in shortening until mixture forms coarse crumbs. Stir in raisins. Add buttermilk and stir until just moistened. Turn onto a lightly floured surface; knead 4 to 5 times. Roll to ½ inch thick and cut with 2½-inch biscuit cutter. Place with sides barely touching on greased baking sheet. Bake 10 to 12 minutes. While still slightly warm, spread with white icing.

White Icing:
Powdered sugar
Milk

Sift a little powdered sugar into a bowl and moisten with cream or milk to spreading consistency. Spread over slightly warm rolls.

Susie Miller
Medford, Wisconsin

> *A good beginning
> is half the job done.*

Light and Tasty Biscuits

2 cups flour

2 ½ teaspoons baking powder

½ teaspoon salt

⅓ cup shortening

¾ cup milk

Butter or margarine

Preheat oven to 475 degrees. Sift together flour, baking powder, and salt. Cut in shortening with fork until mixture resembles coarse cornmeal. Add milk and blend lightly with fork only until flour is moistened and dough pulls away from sides of bowl. Turn out on lightly floured board. Knead lightly (30 seconds) and roll ¾ inch thick. Cut into biscuit shapes. Place on lightly greased baking pan and brush tops with butter or margarine. Bake 12 to 15 minutes.

Mandy R. Schwartz
Portland, Indiana

Johnny Cake

I cup cornmeal
I cup flour
¼ cup sugar
4 teaspoons baking powder
½ teaspoon salt
I cup milk
I egg
¼ cup vegetable oil or lard

Preheat oven to 400 degrees. Mix cornmeal, flour, sugar, baking powder, and salt. Add milk, egg, and oil to dry ingredients and stir only enough to blend. Bake in greased 8x8-inch pan 20 to 25 minutes.

Mrs. Mose J. Byler
New Wilmington, Pennsylvania

♦ ♦ ♦

She who chooses a job she likes will never have to work a day in her life.

♦ ♦ ♦

Esta's Doughnuts

Dough:

4 tablespoons yeast

4 cups lukewarm water

4 pounds raised doughnut mix

Add yeast to lukewarm water. Let set 5 minutes. Add enough doughnut mix so dough will not stick to your hands. Let rise 30 minutes in warm place. Grease flat surface, roll out dough, and cut. Place on baking sheets and let rise in warm place 30 minutes. Deep fry in vegetable shortening at 365 degrees. Glaze while still warm. Yield: 50 large donuts

Glaze:

2 pounds powdered sugar

3 tablespoons butter

2 tablespoons cornstarch

Pinch of salt

1 tablespoon vanilla

Hot water

Mix all ingredients except hot water. Add enough hot water to make glaze to your liking.

Esta Miller
Millersburg, Ohio

Chocolate Chunk Banana Bread

I cup mashed bananas

2 eggs, slightly beaten

⅓ cup oil

¼ cup milk

2 cups flour

I cup sugar

2 teaspoons baking powder

¼ teaspoon salt

I (4 ounce) package Baker's German Sweet Baking
  Chocolate, coarsely chopped

½ cup chopped nuts

Preheat oven to 350 degrees. Stir bananas, eggs, oil, and milk until well blended. Add flour, sugar, baking powder, and salt. Stir until moistened. Stir in chocolate and nuts. Pour into a greased 5x9-inch loaf pan. Bake 55 minutes or until toothpick in center comes out clean. Cool in pan 10 minutes. Remove from pan; cool completely on wire rack.

Janine Merdian
Lacon, Illinois

Maple Twist Rolls

Dough:
¾ cup milk
¼ cup butter
1 tablespoon yeast dissolved
    in ¼ cup warm water
3 tablespoons white sugar
1 egg
½ teaspoon salt
1 teaspoon maple flavoring
2¼ to 3 cups flour

Filling:
¼ cup butter, softened
½ cup brown sugar
½ cup nuts
1 teaspoon cinnamon
1 teaspoon maple flavoring

Frosting:
1 cup powdered sugar
1 tablespoon butter, softened
1 to 2 tablespoons milk
½ teaspoon maple flavoring

Preheat oven to 400 degrees. To make dough, combine milk, butter, yeast dissolved in water, sugar, egg, salt and maple flavoring. Add flour and combine well. Divide dough into three equal balls and roll out. To make filling, combine butter, brown sugar, nuts, cinnamon, and maple flavoring. Spread half of filling on first layer of dough, cover with next layer of dough, and repeat. Put last layer of dough on top. Cut in strips and twist each strip once. Place on baking sheet and let rise. Bake 12 to 15 minutes. To make frosting, combine frosting ingredients and drizzle over top of baked rolls.

Verna Slabaugh
Spickard, Missouri

29

Ice Box Rolls

Dough:

½ cup boiling water

½ cup sugar

¾ teaspoon salt

½ cup shortening

1½ tablespoons yeast

½ cup warm water

1 egg, beaten

3 cups flour

Filling:

2 tablespoons butter, melted

¾ to 1 cup brown sugar

2 teaspoons cinnamon

Preheat oven to 400 degrees. In large bowl, pour boiling water over sugar, salt, and shortening. Set aside to cool. Let yeast stand in warm water until bubbly. Add to sugar mixture; then add beaten egg and flour. Blend well. Grease dough, cover, and let rise in large bowl. (May be stored in refrigerator up to ten days.) Roll out as for cinnamon rolls, spread with melted butter, and sprinkle with brown sugar and cinnamon. Roll up and slice as for rolls. (Note: Dough will be very soft, but do not use more flour. Just flour hands when working with dough.) Place in pans and let rise until light. Bake 12–15 minutes. When cool frost with Quick Icing.

Quick Icing:

3 tablespoons milk

2 tablespoons butter

5 tablespoons brown sugar (⅓ cup)

1 teaspoon vanilla

2 to 3 cups powdered sugar

Warm milk and butter; then mix in brown sugar. Cool and add vanilla and powdered sugar.

Ida Miller
Medford, Wisconsin

Apple Crumb Bread

½ cup butter

1 cup sugar

2 eggs

1 teaspoon baking soda in 2 tablespoons milk

2 cups flour

½ teaspoon salt

1 teaspoon vanilla

1½ cups apples, chopped

Topping:

1 teaspoon cinnamon

2 tablespoons butter

4 tablespoons flour

2 tablespoons brown sugar

Preheat oven to 325 degrees. Cream butter, sugar, and eggs. Add baking soda dissolved in 2 tablespoons milk. Stir in flour, salt, vanilla, and chopped apples. Pour into greased 5½x9-inch bread pan. Combine cinnamon, butter, flour, and brown sugar. Sprinkle on top. Bake 1 hour.

Barbara King
Paradise, Pennsylvania

Mifflin County,
Pennsylvania

In Mifflin County, Pennsylvania, which is located in central Pennsylvania, more than thirteen thousand people live in an area known as the Big Valley. Since 1791 Amish people have lived in the Big Valley, and there are now three different groups of horse-and-buggy Amish who have settled in this area. The Nebraska Amish (an Old Order group that originally came from Nebraska) are the most conservative of these groups. They travel in two-seated buggies with white tops. The Byler (or Old Church) Amish are more progressive and travel in two-seated buggies with yellow tops. The Peachy (or Renno) Amish are the most liberal of the horse-and-buggy Amish living in Mifflin County. They travel in two-seated buggies with black tops.

The majority of these three groups are farmers, and they use draft horses to cultivate the land. All of their farming equipment is mounted on steel wheels. The soil in the Big Valley is rich and full of limestone, which makes for very productive farms. This area's largest industry is still agriculture, partly because of the Amish population living and farming there.

An average of 130 people make up a congregation. They meet for church in one another's homes on a biweekly basis. Usually one bishop, two ministers, and one deacon oversee each congregation.

Despite the differences in the three distinct Amish groups living in Mifflin County, one thing remains the same: All have retained their Amish identity, which is based on a deep religious system that calls for its members to live a life of simplicity, community, peace, and nonconformity.

◆ ◆ ◆

Wisdom is knowing when to speak your mind and when to mind your speech.

◆ ◆ ◆

Breakfast Foods

For where two or three are gathered together in my name,
there am I in the midst of them.

MATTHEW 18:20

Schnitz un Knepp

1 quart dried apples

3 pounds ham

2 tablespoons brown sugar

2 cups flour

1 teaspoon salt

¼ teaspoon pepper

4 teaspoons baking powder

1 egg, well beaten

Milk enough to make a fairly moist, stiff batter

3 tablespoons melted butter

Wash dried apples. Cover with water and let soak overnight or for a number of hours. In the morning, cover ham with cold water in large kettle; then boil 3 hours. Add apples and water in which they have been soaked, and continue to boil for another hour. Add brown sugar. Make dumplings by sifting together flour, salt, pepper, and baking powder. Stir in beaten egg, milk, and butter. Drop batter by spoonfuls into hot liquid around ham and apples. Cover kettle tightly and cook dumplings 15 minutes. Serve piping hot on large platter.

Esther Stauffer
Port Trevorton, Pennsylvania

♦ ♦ ♦

The best reason for doing
what's right today
is tomorrow.

♦ ♦ ♦

Creamed Eggs

White Sauce:
4 tablespoons butter
4 tablespoons flour
½ teaspoon salt
2 cups milk

5 eggs, hard boiled
2 cups medium white sauce
5 slices hot, buttered toast

Melt butter in heavy saucepan. Blend in flour and salt, cooking and stirring until bubbly. Using a wire whisk, stir in milk. Cook just until smooth and thickened.

Shell eggs, slice, and fold them into the hot white sauce so as not to break up the eggs. Pour over hot, buttered toast.

Sam Schwartz
Portland, Indiana

*A thousand words will
not leave so deep an
impression as one deed.*

Country Breakfast

14 slices bread
2½ cups cubed ham
1 pound mozzarella cheese,
    shredded
1 pound cheddar cheese, shredded
6 eggs
3 cups milk

Topping:
½ cup butter, melted
3 cups cornflakes (do not crush)

Preheat oven to 375 degrees. Grease 9x13-inch pan and layer half of bread, ham, and cheese. Repeat layers. Beat eggs, add milk, and pour over layers. Refrigerate overnight. Mix butter and cornflakes, and add topping just before baking. Cover loosely with foil and bake 45 minutes.

Sara Blank
Narvon, Pennsylvania

CECIL COUNTY
PUBLIC LIBRARY
301 Newark Ave.
Elkton, MD 21921

Country Brunch Skillet

6 strips bacon
6 cups cubed hash brown potatoes
¾ cup green pepper, chopped
½ cup onion, chopped
1 teaspoon salt
¼ teaspoon pepper
6 eggs, beaten
½ cup cheddar cheese, shredded

Cook bacon. Remove from pan. Brown potatoes in bacon grease. Add green pepper, onion, salt, and pepper. Stir-fry until almost done; then pour eggs over top. Stir in cheese and cook until done. Crumble bacon on top.

Katie H. Zook
Apple Creek, Ohio

Omelet Sandwiches

16 slices bread (buttered on one side)
1 pound shaved ham
8 slices cheese
6 eggs
3 cups milk
½ teaspoon mustard
½ teaspoon salt
1 cup cornflakes, crushed
½ cup butter, melted

Preheat oven to 350 degrees. Make eight sandwiches with bread, ham, and cheese. Put in greased baking dish. Mix eggs, milk, mustard, and salt. Pour over sandwiches. Refrigerate overnight. In the morning, mix cornflakes and butter; sprinkle on top. Bake 1 hour. Yield: 8 large servings

Heidi S. Stauffer
Homer City, Pennsylvania

Brunch

4 eggs

2 cups milk

½ teaspoon salt

¼ teaspoon dry mustard

½ teaspoon onion salt

6 strips bacon, cooked and crumbled
    (or ½ pound sausage, cooked)

2 cups toasted bread crumbs

1 cup grated cheese

Preheat oven to 325 degrees. Grease 7x11-inch pan. Beat eggs, milk, and seasonings. Crumble bacon or sausage into egg and milk mixture. Put toasted bread crumbs on bottom of pan. Layer with grated cheese; then pour in egg mixture. Bake 50 minutes. Serves 4 or more.

Barbara L. Weaver
Osseo, Michigan

*Expert opinion is rarely
as good as common sense.*

Butterscotch Granola

10 cups oatmeal

2 packages graham crackers, crushed

2 cups coconut, flaked

1 cup pecans, chopped

¾ cup brown sugar

1 teaspoon soda

1 teaspoon salt

2 cups margarine or butter, melted

1 cup mini butterscotch chips

Preheat oven to 300 degrees. Grease large baking pan. Mix all dry ingredients except chips. Add melted butter. Bake 40 minutes, stirring every 10 minutes. Add chips during last few minutes before removing from oven. Cool. Yield: 5 quarts

Mrs. Andrew J. Hostetler
Homerville, Ohio

Pancake Syrup

1¼ cups brown sugar

½ cup light corn syrup

1 cup water

¾ cup sugar

1 teaspoon vanilla

½ teaspoon maple flavoring (optional)

Bring brown sugar, corn syrup, water, and sugar to a boil, stirring constantly. Simmer on low heat 5 minutes. Remove from heat and add vanilla. Maple flavoring may be added.

Katie Schwartz
Marlette, Michigan

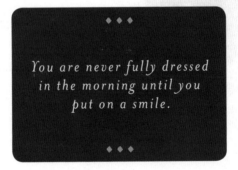

You are never fully dressed in the morning until you put on a smile.

Cheese Potato Breakfast Casserole

2 pounds frozen hash browns, thawed
½ cup margarine or butter, melted
1 teaspoon salt
¼ teaspoon pepper
1 (10¾ ounce) can of cream of chicken soup
2 cups sour cream
2 cups cheddar cheese, grated
½ cup onion, chopped

Topping:
2 cups cornflakes, crushed
¼ cup margarine or butter, melted

Preheat oven to 350 degrees. Combine all ingredients except topping. Pour into greased 9x13-inch baking dish. Cover with topping. Bake 45 to 50 minutes.

Esther A. Hershberger
Goshen, Indiana

Overnight Breakfast Casserole

8 slices bread, cubed

¾ pound cheese, shredded

1½ pounds pork sausage or 1 quart canned sausage

4 eggs

2½ cups milk

1 tablespoon prepared mustard

1 (10¾ ounce) can cream of mushroom
    or cream of chicken soup

¼ cup chicken broth

Preheat oven to 350 degrees. Place bread cubes in ungreased baking dish. Sprinkle with cheese. Set aside. In skillet, brown sausage over medium heat; drain fat. Crumble sausage over cheese and bread. (If using canned sausage, just crumble.) Beat eggs, milk, mustard, soup, and broth. Pour over sausage. Cover and refrigerate overnight or at least 2 or 3 hours before baking. Bake 50 to 60 minutes or until done.

Mrs. Abner Z. Fisher
Aaronsburg, Pennsylvania

Honey French Toast

2 eggs, well beaten
¼ cup milk
¼ cup honey
¼ teaspoon salt
6 to 8 slices of bread
Butter

Combine eggs, milk, honey, and salt. Dip bread slices into honey mixture. Fry in butter over medium heat on both sides until golden brown.

Mrs. Joe J. Miller
Lakeview, Michigan

Buckwheat Pancakes

2 cups buckwheat flour
1 teaspoon salt
3 teaspoons baking powder
⅓ teaspoon baking soda
¼ cup oil
1 egg
1 cup sour milk
½ cup water

Combine all ingredients. Fry in a greased skillet. Turn over once. Serve with butter and honey, gravy, or jelly. If desired, add blueberries to the batter.

Esther Stauffer
Port Trevorton, Pennsylvania

Apple Pancakes

1 cup pancake mix

1 egg

¾ cup milk

2 tablespoons salad oil

¼ cup butter

⅓ cup brown sugar

1 to 2 apples, peeled and sliced

Combine pancake mix, egg, milk, and oil. Melt butter and brown sugar in iron skillet and spread sliced apples over bottom of pan in brown sugar mixture. Pour pancake batter over apples and bake until set.

Maria Schrock
Princeton, Missouri

Laughter is the jam on the toast of life. It adds flavor, keeps it from becoming too dry, and makes it easier to swallow.

Breakfast Pizza Delight

1½ pounds sausage
1½ cups pizza sauce
12 slices bread
12 slices cheese
3 cups milk
1 teaspoon salt
5 eggs

Fry meat, drain fat, and add pizza sauce. Preheat oven to 350 degrees. In 9x13-inch pan, top 6 slices bread with 6 slices cheese. Add meat mixture, rest of cheese, and remaining bread. Beat together milk, salt, and eggs and pour over bread. Bake 35 to 45 minutes or until done and golden brown.

Elva Shirk
Dundee, New York

Holmes County, Ohio

A group of Old Order Amish first settled in Holmes County, Ohio, at the beginning of the nineteenth century. In the years since, their numbers have grown, spilling into nearby Wayne, Tuscarawas, Coshocton, Knox, and Ashland counties. This area of Ohio contains the largest Amish population in America.

Even though there is some tourism and a growing number of non-Amish commercial enterprises, the Holmes County region is virtually unspoiled. When you drive through Holmes County and the surrounding areas, you will share the road with black Amish buggies, iron-wheeled wagons, and pony carts. Well-maintained Amish homes and gardens can be seen throughout much of the area.

Outsiders visiting Holmes County will often see Amish families at local restaurants, and many fast-food restaurants even have hitching rails for buggies in their parking lots. The Amish in Holmes County and the surrounding counties are generally quite friendly to their neighbors and outsiders as well.

The soil is rich in Holmes County, and while some Amish still farm for a living, there are many others who have home-based businesses, which they use either to support their families or to supplement their incomes. There are several Amish furniture shops in the region, as well as bulk-food stores, quilt shops, bakeries, buggy shops, and harness shops. On Wednesdays there is a livestock sale in Mount Hope, and on Fridays a horse sale is held in Sugarcreek that attracts hundreds of local Amish and Englishers alike.

# Desserts

*And we know that all things work together for good to them that love God,
to them who are the called according to his purpose.*

ROMANS 8:28

Easy Strawberry Shortcake

2 cups flour
1 cup sugar
⅓ cup butter
½ teaspoon soda
1 cup buttermilk
2 tablespoons sugar
1 tablespoon flour

Preheat oven to 350 degrees. In large bowl, use spoon (not electric mixer) to combine flour, sugar, butter, soda, and buttermilk. Pour into greased 9x9-inch pan. Sprinkle top with sugar and flour mixture. Bake 30 to 35 minutes.

Susie Knepp
Montgomery, Indiana

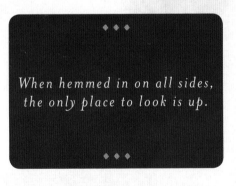

When hemmed in on all sides, the only place to look is up.

Cherry Coffee Cake

1 cup margarine

1½ cups sugar

4 eggs, well beaten

1 teaspoon vanilla

3 cups flour

1½ teaspoons baking powder

½ teaspoon salt

1 can cherry pie filling

Glaze:

1½ cups powdered sugar

2 tablespoons melted butter

Milk—enough to make a thin consistency

Preheat oven to 350 degrees. Cream margarine and sugar. Add well-beaten eggs and vanilla. Sift and add dry ingredients. Spread two-thirds of dough in greased 9x9-inch pan. Cover with cherry pie filling. Drop spoonfuls of remaining dough over the top. Bake 30 to 40 minutes. Mix glaze ingredients and drizzle over warm coffee cake.

Mrs. Crist Schrock
Sullivan, Ohio

Coconut Pecan Frosting

I cup evaporated milk or cream

I cup sugar

3 egg yolks

2 tablespoons margarine or butter

I teaspoon vanilla

1⅓ cups coconut

I cup pecans, chopped

Stirring constantly, cook milk, sugar, egg yolks, margarine, and vanilla over medium heat 12 minutes or until thickened. Cool. Add coconut and pecans. Beat until thick enough to spread.

Mrs. Harvey R. Miller
South Dayton, New York

Fluffy Cocoa Frosting

2 cups powdered sugar

⅛ cup cocoa

¼ cup butter

¼ cup cream

I teaspoon vanilla

Beat all ingredients until fluffy.

Martha Yoder
Crofton, Kentucky

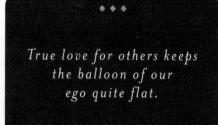

True love for others keeps
the balloon of our
ego quite flat.

Buttermilk Coconut Cake

2 cups sugar
4 eggs
1 cup buttermilk
1 cup oil
1 cup coconut, shredded
1½ teaspoons coconut flavoring
2 cups self-rising flour

Preheat oven to 350 degrees. Mix sugar, eggs, buttermilk, oil, coconut, and flavoring. Add flour and mix well. Bake in greased Bundt pan 1 hour.

Glaze:
1 cup sugar
⅓ cup water
1 teaspoon coconut flakes

Combine glaze ingredients and boil 2 minutes. Pour glaze over hot cake.

Charlene Wenger
Elkhorn, Kentucky

Texas Sheet Cake

2 cups bread flour

2 cups sugar

1 cup margarine or butter, melted

3 tablespoons cocoa

1 cup water

2 eggs, beaten

½ cup sour milk

1 teaspoon baking soda

¼ teaspoon salt

1 teaspoon vanilla

Preheat oven to 350 degrees. Combine flour and sugar in mixing bowl. Stir together melted margarine and cocoa and add water. Bring to a boil. Pour over flour and sugar mixture. Add eggs, sour milk, baking soda, salt, and vanilla. Mix well. Pour into a greased 10x15x1-inch baking sheet. Bake 25 minutes or until done. Frost cake and sprinkle with chopped nuts.

Frosting:

3 tablespoons cocoa

½ cup margarine or butter

6 tablespoons milk

1 teaspoon vanilla

1 pound (3½ cups) powdered sugar

1 cup nuts, chopped

Stir cocoa into melted margarine. Add milk and vanilla. Pour over powdered sugar and mix well.

Mrs. Leander Miller
Cashton, Wisconsin

Honey Bun Cake

1 yellow cake mix

4 eggs

⅔ cup oil

½ cup sour cream

1 cup brown sugar

2 teaspoons cinnamon

Glaze:

1½ cups powdered sugar

2 teaspoons vanilla

⅓ to ½ cup milk

Preheat oven to 350 degrees. Combine cake mix, eggs, oil, and sour cream. Beat 3 minutes. Pour ½ of mixture into greased 9x13-inch pan. Mix together brown sugar and cinnamon and sprinkle over mixture in pan. Drizzle on other half of batter. Bake 45 to 60 minutes. Poke holes in cake with fork. Mix glaze ingredients and pour over cake while still warm.

Saloma Slabaugh
Spickard, Missouri

• • •

Half of our lives are spent trying to find something to do with the time we have rushed through life trying to save.

• • •

Chocolate Chip Date Nut Cake

1½ cups boiling water
1 cup dates, finely chopped
1¾ teaspoons baking soda, divided
½ cup butter, softened
1½ cups sugar
2 eggs
1½ cups flour
½ teaspoon salt
1 cup (6 ounces) chocolate chips
¾ cup walnuts, chopped

Preheat oven to 350 degrees. In small bowl, combine water, dates, and 1 teaspoon soda. Cool completely. In large bowl, cream butter and 1 cup sugar. Add eggs, one at a time, beating well after each addition. Combine flour, salt, and remaining baking soda; add to creamed mixture alternately with date mixture. Batter will be thin. Pour into greased 9x13-inch pan. Combine chocolate chips, walnuts, and remaining ½ cup sugar. Sprinkle over batter. Bake 30 to 35 minutes or until toothpick inserted in center comes out clean. Cool on wire rack.

Mrs. Joseph Zook
Rebersburg, Pennsylvania

Caramel Apple Crunch Cake

1½ cups cooking oil

3 eggs

2 cups sugar

2 teaspoons vanilla

3 cups flour

1½ teaspoons soda

1 teaspoon salt

1 cup walnuts, chopped

1 cup coconut

3 cups apples, chopped

Preheat oven to 350 degrees. Combine oil, eggs, sugar, and vanilla in bowl. Add flour, soda, and salt. Mix well. Stir in walnuts, coconut, and apples. Pour into greased tube pan. Bake 1½ hours.

Icing:

1 stick (½ cup) butter

1 cup brown sugar

¼ cup milk

Boil butter, brown sugar, and milk in saucepan 2½ minutes. Pour icing over cake while still hot. Leave cake in pan until cool then place on plate.

Martha Yoder
Harrisville, Pennsylvania

Dump Cake

1 cup cherry pie filling
1 can (15½ ounce) crushed pineapple, undrained
1 yellow cake mix
1 cup nuts, chopped
1 cup coconut, flaked
2 sticks margarine, melted

Preheat oven to 350 degrees. Spread pie filling and pineapple in ungreased 9x12-inch pan. Sprinkle dry cake mix over fruit. Top evenly with nuts and coconut. Drizzle melted margarine over all. Bake 70 minutes. Cool completely before cutting.

Mrs. Andrew J. Hostetler
Homerville, Ohio

Maple Pudding Cake

1 cup flour

2 teaspoons baking powder

¼ teaspoon salt

½ cup sugar

½ cup milk

2 tablespoons butter or softened shortening

1 cup nuts, chopped

1 cup maple syrup

¾ cup boiling water

Whipped cream

Preheat oven to 350 degrees. In large bowl, combine flour, baking powder, salt, and sugar. Mix in milk and butter. Stir in nuts. Spread batter in 2-quart baking dish. Combine maple syrup and boiling water. Pour over batter. Bake 40 to 45 minutes. The cake will rise to the top, and the sauce will settle to the bottom. Serve warm with whipped cream.

Susie Miller
Medford, Wisconsin

♦ ♦ ♦

Good, better, best. . .never let it rest until the good is better and the better is best.

♦ ♦ ♦

Mexican Chocolate Chiffon Cake

¾ cup hot coffee

⅓ cup cocoa

1¾ cups cake flour

1⅔ cups white sugar

1½ teaspoons soda

½ teaspoon salt

½ cup vegetable oil

7 egg yolks

1 teaspoon vanilla

7 egg whites

½ teaspoon cream of tartar

Preheat oven to 325 degrees. Blend hot coffee and cocoa. Let cool. Sift flour, sugar, soda, and salt into bowl. Make a well in center and add oil, yolks, vanilla, and coffee mixture. Beat until smooth. In large bowl, beat egg whites and cream of tartar until very stiff. Pour chocolate mixture over egg whites and fold in gently. Put into ungreased tube pan. Bake 55 minutes at 325 degrees then increase temperature to 350 degrees for 10 to 15 minutes.

Katie Wenger
Bainbridge, Ohio

Fruit Cake

1 cup cooking oil

1⅓ cups sugar

¼ cup molasses

4 eggs

2 cups sifted flour

1 teaspoon baking powder

1 teaspoon salt

2 teaspoons cinnamon

2 teaspoons nutmeg

1 cup fresh orange juice

1 cup flour

2⅔ cups seedless raisins

1 cup English walnuts

2 cups dates, cut up

2 cups mixed candied fruit

Preheat oven to 275 degrees. Mix oil, sugar, molasses, and eggs. Beat 2 minutes. Sift together 2 cups flour, baking powder, salt, and spices. Stir in alternately with sugar mixture and orange juice. Mix 1 cup flour with raisins, nuts, dates, and fruit. Add to batter, mixing thoroughly. Pour into lightly greased tube pan. Bake 2 to 2½ hours. Let cool in pan 1 hour before removing.

Lydia A. Yoder
Rome, Pennsylvania

Quick Caramel Frosting

½ cup butter

I cup brown sugar, firmly packed

¼ cup milk

I¾ to 2 cups powdered sugar

Melt butter and add brown sugar. Cook over low heat 2 minutes, stirring constantly. Add milk and continue stirring until mixture comes to a boil. Remove from heat and cool. Beat in powdered sugar until frosting is right consistency to spread.

Kathy Renee Miller
Guthrie, Kentucky

Caramels

2 cups white sugar
1¾ cups molasses
2 cups cream
1 cup butter
1 teaspoon vanilla

Mix sugar, molasses, half of cream, butter, and vanilla. Bring to a boil over low heat, stirring constantly. Add remaining cream. Don't allow boiling to stop. Boil until piece of mixture forms firm ball in cold water (250 degrees). Pour into buttered 9x9-inch pan. When cool cut in squares and wrap in waxed paper.

Naomi Smoker
Myerstown, Pennsylvania

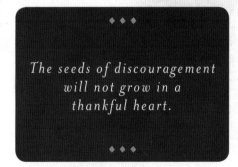

The seeds of discouragement will not grow in a thankful heart.

Million Dollar Fudge

1 cup chopped nuts
1 (12 ounce) package chocolate chips
1 (10¾ ounce) chocolate bar
2 cups marshmallow creme
1 teaspoon vanilla
4 cups sugar
1 (13 ounce) can evaporated milk

In large bowl, combine nuts, chocolate chips, chocolate bar, marshmallow creme, and vanilla. Bring sugar and milk to a boil in saucepan, stirring constantly. Boil 7 to 10 minutes. Pour over mixture in bowl. Stir until all ingredients are melted. Pour into 2 buttered 8- or 9-inch square pans. When set cut into squares. Yield: 5 pounds

Mary A. Schlabach
Smicksburg, Pennsylvania

No-Cook Fudge

2 cups powdered sugar, sifted
1 (8 ounce) package cream cheese, softened
4 ounces unsweetened chocolate, melted
½ cup walnuts or pecans, chopped
1 teaspoon vanilla
Dash of salt

Gradually add powdered sugar to softened cream cheese and mix well.
Thoroughly mix in warm chocolate. Stir in nuts. Add vanilla and salt.
Spread in greased 8x8-inch pan. Cut and serve.

Mrs. Levi Stutzman
West Salem, Ohio

When we climb the steep
mountains of life, we get a
better view of the blessings.

Peanut Brittle

½ cup butter
1 cup light corn syrup
1 cup white sugar
3 cups peanuts
2 teaspoons soda

Combine butter, corn syrup, and sugar and cook to soft ball stage (240 degrees). Pour in peanuts and stir. Cook until candy thermometer reaches hard crack stage (300 degrees). Take off heat and quickly mix in soda. It will foam up. Pour over foil and let cool before breaking up.

Saloma Slabaugh
Spickard, Missouri

Buckeyes

1 (12 ounce) package chocolate chips
⅓ stick paraffin
1 pound powdered sugar
1 stick margarine, softened
2 cups peanut butter
3 cups crisp rice cereal

Melt chocolate chips and paraffin over low heat. Set aside. Combine sugar, margarine, peanut butter, and crisp rice cereal. Form into small balls and dip in melted chocolate and paraffin.

Barbara L. Weaver
Osseo, Michigan

White Chocolate Candy

1 pound white chocolate
1 cup creamy peanut butter
1 cup pecans or walnuts, chopped

Melt chocolate over hot water. Stir in peanut butter and nuts. Pour into 8x8-inch pan lined with waxed paper. When cool remove from pan. Remove paper and cut into squares.

Rebecca Troyer
Berne, Indiana

Mints

1 (8 ounce) package cream cheese
2 pounds powdered sugar
Color paste (amount according to color desired)
Mint flavoring (according to taste)
1 cup white sugar

Divide cream cheese into two equal parts and bring to room temperature. To each 4-ounce portion of cream cheese, add 1 pound of powdered sugar and knead. Add color paste with toothpick and a few drops of flavoring. Work into dough and taste for correct amount of flavor. Form into shapes or roll into balls then roll in sugar and press into molds. A food processor can be used to make this dough. Yield: 180 mints

Rosanna Zimmerman
New Holland, Pennsylvania

Cherries 'n Chocolate Fudge

1 (14 ounce) can sweetened condensed milk
2 cups (12 ounces) semisweet chocolate chips
½ cup almonds, coarsely chopped
½ cup candied cherries, chopped
1 teaspoon almond extract

Line an 8x8-inch pan with foil. In medium saucepan, combine condensed milk and chocolate chips. Heat until chocolate chips are melted. Stir in almonds, cherries, and almond extract. Spread evenly in pan. Cover and chill until firm. Cut into 1-inch squares. Store covered in refrigerator. Yield: about 4 dozen squares

Janine Merdian
Lacon, Illinois

God owes us nothing,
but He gives us everything.

Rocky Road Candy

½ cup butter or margarine
½ cup powdered sugar
1 egg, beaten
1 cup chocolate or butterscotch chips
3 or 4 cups miniature marshmallows
10 graham cracker squares

Combine butter, powdered sugar, egg, and chocolate chips. Heat in double boiler. Stir until melted. Cool slightly. Add marshmallows. Line bottom of ungreased 8x8-inch pan with graham crackers. Pour melted mixture on top. Cool. Cut into squares.

Barbara Miller
Port Washington, Ohio

Date Balls

1 egg, beaten
1 cup sugar
1 stick butter or margarine
1 cup dates, cut up
3 cups crisp rice cereal
1–2 cups coconut, flaked

Combine beaten egg, sugar, butter, and dates in saucepan. Cook slowly 6 minutes. Pour over crisp rice cereal and stir. Shape into balls then roll in coconut.

Mrs. Eli Miller
Chili, Wisconsin

Peanut Butter Fingers

½ cup butter or margarine
½ cup white sugar
½ cup brown sugar
1 egg
⅓ cup peanut butter
½ teaspoon soda
¼ teaspoon salt
½ teaspoon vanilla
1 cup rolled oats
1 cup flour
1 (6 ounce) package chocolate chips

Preheat oven to 350 degrees. Cream butter and sugars. Blend in egg and peanut butter. Add soda, salt, vanilla, oats, and flour. Mix well. Bake in greased 9x13-inch pan 20 to 25 minutes. Spread chocolate chips over the top while still hot. Cool. Frost with Peanut Butter Frosting. Cut into bars for serving.

Peanut Butter Frosting:
½ cup powdered sugar
¼ cup peanut butter
2 to 4 tablespoons milk

Combine sugar and peanut butter and stir in milk until it reaches the desired spreading consistency.

Amanda Stutzman
Apple Creek, Ohio

Butterscotch Cheese Bars

⅓ cup butter

8 ounces butterscotch chips

2 cups graham cracker crumbs

1 cup nuts, chopped

1 (8 ounce) package cream cheese, softened

1 egg

1 teaspoon vanilla

1 can (14 ounces) sweetened condensed milk

Preheat oven to 350 degrees. Melt butter and butterscotch chips. Add graham cracker crumbs and nuts. Mix well and press half of crumb mixture into greased 9x13-inch pan. Combine cream cheese, egg, vanilla, and condensed milk and pour over crumbs. Add rest of crumbs on top. Bake 25 to 30 minutes.

Sharon Zimmerman
Port Trevorton, Pennsylvania

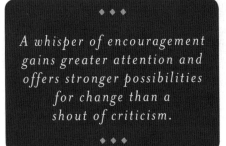

♦ ♦ ♦

A whisper of encouragement gains greater attention and offers stronger possibilities for change than a shout of criticism.

♦ ♦ ♦

Bill Bars

1 chocolate cake mix
1 egg
⅓ cup oil
1 (8 ounce) package cream cheese, softened
⅓ cup sugar
1 egg
1 cup chocolate chips

Preheat oven to 350 degrees. Mix cake mix, egg, and oil by hand until crumbly. Reserve 1 cup for topping. Press remaining crumb mixture into ungreased 9x13-inch pan. Bake 15 minutes. Cool slightly. Beat cream cheese, sugar, and egg until fluffy. Spread over baked layer. Sprinkle chocolate chips and reserved 1 cup crumb mixture over the top. Bake 15 minutes more.

Sarah B. Eicher
Geneva, Indiana

Moonlight Bars

½ cup white sugar
½ cup light corn syrup
1 teaspoon vanilla
1 cup peanut butter
2 tablespoons margarine
3 cups cornflakes

In heavy pan, combine sugar and light corn syrup. Heat on low heat until sugar is dissolved, stirring vigorously and constantly. Do not allow to boil. Remove from heat and add vanilla, peanut butter, margarine, and cornflakes. Mix well and put in greased 8x8-inch pan. When cool cut into squares.

Susie A. Miller
Dundee, Ohio

◆ ◆ ◆

A friend is a precious possession whose value increases with years, someone who doesn't forsake us when difficult moments appear.

◆ ◆ ◆

Maple Chocolate Walnut Bars

Crust:

1½ cups flour

⅔ cup sugar

¾ cup cold butter or margarine

½ teaspoon salt

1 egg, beaten

Preheat oven to 350 degrees. In large bowl, mix flour, sugar, butter, and salt until crumbly. Stir in beaten egg. Press evenly into greased 9x13-inch pan. Bake 25 minutes.

Filling:

1 cup chocolate chips

1 (14 ounce) can sweetened condensed milk

1½ teaspoons maple flavoring

1 egg, beaten

2 cups walnuts, chopped

Sprinkle chocolate chips over baked crust. Combine condensed milk, flavoring, and egg, and stir in walnuts. Pour over baked crust and bake 20 minutes longer or until golden brown. Cool. Cut into bars.

Alice Beechy
Pittsford, Michigan

Lemon Bars

1 cup butter or margarine
2 cups flour
½ cup powdered sugar
Pinch of salt

Preheat oven to 350 degrees. Mix butter, flour, powdered sugar, and salt. Pat into 9x13-inch pan. Bake 15 to 20 minutes.

Filling:
4 eggs, beaten
2 cups white sugar
6 tablespoons lemon juice
4 tablespoons flour

Topping:
¼ to ½ cup powdered sugar

Beat eggs, sugar, lemon juice, and flour. Pour over baked crust and bake 20 to 30 minutes more. Sprinkle powdered sugar lightly over top after removing from oven.

Emma E. Raber
Holmesville, Ohio

Chocolate Pecan Cheesecake Bars

Crust:

1 chocolate cake mix

½ cup margarine, softened

1 egg

½ cup pecans, chopped

Filling:

1 (8 ounce) package cream cheese, softened

1 (14 ounce) can sweetened condensed milk

1 egg

1 teaspoon vanilla

Preheat oven to 350 degrees. Grease 9x13-inch pan. Combine cake mix, margarine, egg, and pecans in bowl. Reserve 1 cup for topping. Press remaining mixture evenly in pan. Beat cream cheese until fluffy. Add milk, egg, and vanilla. Beat until smooth. Pour over crust. Sprinkle with reserved topping. Bake 35 to 40 minutes or until center is puffed and edges are lightly browned.

Mary Schlabach
Smicksburg, Pennsylvania

> ◆ ◆ ◆
>
> *Experience is a hard teacher.*
> *She gives the test first and*
> *the lesson afterward.*
>
> ◆ ◆ ◆

In youth we learn;
in age we understand.

Apple Bars

6 cups apples, peeled and chopped
4 cups flour
1 teaspoon salt
2 cups sugar
1 cup margarine
2 teaspoons cinnamon, divided

Preheat oven to 350 degrees. Peel and chop apples to measure 6 cups
and set aside. Mix flour, salt, and sugar. Add margarine and mix to make
crumbs (makes about 7½ cups crumbs). Mix ½ cup crumbs and 1 teaspoon
of cinnamon into apples; set aside. Divide the rest of the crumbs in half
and place in a greased 9x13-inch pan. Press down lightly. Bake 10 minutes.
Remove from oven. Top with apples and remaining crumbs. Sprinkle with
1 teaspoon cinnamon. Bake 40 minutes more. Cool and cut into bars.

Mary Miller
Heuvelton, New York

Pecan Squares

Crust:

3 cups flour

½ cup sugar

1 cup butter or margarine, softened

½ teaspoon salt

Filling:

4 eggs

1½ cups light or dark corn syrup

1½ cups sugar

3 tablespoons butter or margarine, melted

1½ teaspoons vanilla

2½ cups pecans, chopped

Preheat oven to 350 degrees. Blend flour, sugar, butter, and salt until mixture forms coarse crumbs. Press into greased 9x13-inch pan. Bake 20 minutes. Meanwhile, combine eggs, corn syrup, sugar, butter, and vanilla. Stir in pecans. Spread filling evenly over hot crust and bake another 25 minutes or until set. Cool and cut into squares. Store in airtight container. Yield: 2 dozen

Mary Schwartz
Monroe, Indiana

Apple Butter Bars

1½ cups flour
1 teaspoon soda
1 teaspoon salt
2½ cups oats
1½ cups sugar
1 cup margarine
1½ cups apple butter

Preheat oven to 350 degrees. Sift together flour, soda, and salt in large bowl. Add oats and sugar. Stir in margarine and mix well. Press half of mixture in bottom of greased 9x13-inch pan. Top with apple butter. Sprinkle with remaining crumbs; press gently with spoon. Bake 55 minutes or until brown.

Nelson and Miriam Hershberger
Calhoun, Illinois

Marbled Chocolate Bars

1 German chocolate cake mix
1 (8 ounce) package cream cheese, softened
½ cup sugar
¾ cup milk chocolate chips, divided

Preheat oven to 350 degrees. Prepare cake batter according to package directions. Pour into greased 10x15x1-inch pan. In small mixing bowl, beat cream cheese and sugar. Stir in ¼ cup chocolate chips. Drop cheese mixture by tablespoonfuls over batter. Cut through batter with knife to swirl cream cheese mixture. Sprinkle with remaining chocolate chips. Bake 25 to 30 minutes or until a toothpick inserted in center comes out clean.

Rose Marie Shetler
Berne, Indiana

Black and White
Cream Cheese Bars

2 cups chocolate chips

½ cup margarine

2 cups graham cracker crumbs

1 (8 ounce) package cream cheese, softened

1 (14 ounce) can sweetened condensed milk

1 egg

1 teaspoon vanilla

Preheat oven to 375 degrees. Melt chocolate chips and margarine. Stir in graham cracker crumbs. Set ¼ cup aside for topping. Press remaining crumbs in greased 9x13-inch pan. Beat cream cheese until smooth and gradually beat in condensed milk, egg, and vanilla. Pour over crust. Sprinkle with remaining crumbs. Bake 25 to 30 minutes or until lightly browned.

Lizzie Schwartz
Geneva, Indiana

Mound Bars

2 cups graham crackers, crushed
½ cup butter, melted
¼ cup sugar
1 (14 ounce) can sweetened condensed milk
½ cup coconut
6 ounces chocolate chips

Preheat oven to 350 degrees. Combine cracker crumbs, butter, and sugar.
Press in 9x13-inch pan. Bake 15 minutes. Combine milk and coconut.
Spread over baked layer. Bake another 15 minutes. Melt chocolate chips and
spread over baked bars.

Ida J. Miller
Medford, Wisconsin

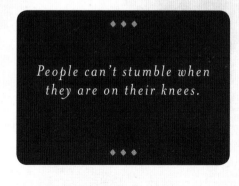

*People can't stumble when
they are on their knees.*

Coffee Bars

2⅔ cups brown sugar

1 cup vegetable oil

1 cup warm coffee (made with
    1 teaspoon instant coffee)

1 teaspoon salt

1 teaspoon soda

1 teaspoon vanilla

2 eggs

3 cups flour

1 cup nuts, chopped

1 cup chocolate chips

Preheat oven to 350 degrees. Combine brown sugar, oil, coffee, salt, soda, vanilla, eggs, flour, and nuts. Beat well. Pour into greased 9x13-inch pan and sprinkle with chocolate chips. Bake 25 to 30 minutes.

Verna Miller
Apple Creek, Ohio

Jell-O Cookies

2½ cups flour

1 teaspoon soda

½ teaspoon salt

¾ cup butter

¾ cup sugar

1 teaspoon vanilla

3 ounces dry gelatin
(use your favorite flavor)

2 eggs

½ cup milk

Preheat oven to 375 degrees. Sift together flour, soda, and salt. Cream butter, sugar, and vanilla. Add gelatin and eggs, one at a time, and beat well with milk. Combine creamed mixture with flour mixture. Drop heaping teaspoons on greased baking sheet and bake 10 minutes. When cool frost with your favorite powdered sugar frosting.

Mrs. Joe J. Miller
Lakeview, Michigan

Boyfriend Cookies

1 cup butter, softened
¾ cup granulated sugar
¾ cup brown sugar, packed
3 eggs
1 teaspoon vanilla
¼ cup whole-wheat flour
¼ cup soy flour
3½ cups quick-cooking oatmeal
1½ cups salted peanuts, coarsely chopped
1 cup carob chips

Preheat oven to 350 degrees. Cream butter and sugars. Add eggs and vanilla, beating until fluffy. Sift flours and add to creamed mixture. Fold in oatmeal, peanuts, and carob chips. Drop by teaspoon onto greased baking sheet and bake 8 to 10 minutes. Yield: 7 to 8 dozen

Emma A. Troyer
New Wilmington, Pennsylvania

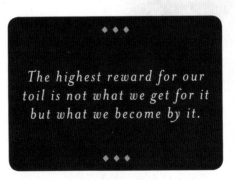

The highest reward for our toil is not what we get for it but what we become by it.

Date Pinwheel Cookies

Filling:

2 pounds dates, chopped

1 cup white sugar

1 cup water

In saucepan combine dates, white sugar, and water. Cook over medium-low heat, stirring constantly until a smooth paste is formed. Remove from heat and cool.

Dough:

1⅓ cups brown sugar

⅔ cup shortening

2 eggs, beaten

2½ cups flour

¾ teaspoon baking soda

½ teaspoon salt

½ teaspoon cinnamon

Preheat oven to 400 degrees. Cream brown sugar and shortening. Add eggs and beat until mixture is light and fluffy. Combine flour, baking soda, salt, and cinnamon. Gradually add to creamed mixture and mix well. Stir until soft dough forms. Divide dough into 4 parts. Cover with waxed paper and chill dough thoroughly. Working one piece at a time, keep the rest of the dough cool; roll the dough out in a rectangle ⅛-inch thick. Spread dough with date filling to within ¼ inch of the edges then roll up jelly-roll style, starting with a long side. Pinch edge to seal. Wrap each roll and refrigerate overnight. Remove from refrigerator as you need them. With a sharp knife, cut in ¼-inch slices and bake on lightly greased baking sheet 8 to 10 minutes or until light golden brown.

Susan Weaver
Osseo, Michigan

> *Every tomorrow has two*
> *handles. We can grasp*
> *the handle of anxiety or*
> *the handle of faith.*

Swedish Butter Cookies

1 cup butter, softened (no substitutes)
1 cup sugar
2 teaspoons maple syrup
2 cups flour
1 teaspoon baking soda

Preheat oven to 300 degrees. Cream butter and sugar. Add syrup and stir well. Combine flour and soda and add to creamed mixture. Roll into balls and place on ungreased baking sheet. Bake 25 minutes or until lightly browned.

Linda E. Peachey
Beaver, Ohio

Maple Nut Cookies

2 cups brown sugar
1 cup butter
3 eggs
1¼ tablespoons maple flavoring
¾ cup milk
4 cups flour
2 teaspoons soda
¼ teaspoon salt
¾ cup nuts, chopped

Preheat oven to 350 degrees. Cream brown sugar and butter. Add eggs, flavoring, and milk. Beat well. Combine flour, soda, and salt. Add to creamed mixture. Fold in nuts. Drop by heaping teaspoons onto greased baking sheet and bake 8 to 10 minutes. Frost cookies when cooled.

Frosting:
¼ cup butter
1 egg, beaten
1 teaspoon maple flavoring
2¼ cups powdered sugar
2 teaspoons water

Combine butter, egg, flavoring, powdered sugar, and water. Mix well.

Lizzie Yoder
Fredericksburg, Ohio

Banana Whoopie Pie Cookies

2 cups brown sugar

1 cup shortening

2 eggs

2 cups bananas, mashed

1 teaspoon vanilla

3½ cups flour

1 teaspoon baking soda

1 teaspoon salt

1 teaspoon baking powder

½ teaspoon cinnamon

½ teaspoon ginger

Preheat oven to 350 degrees. Cream brown sugar and shortening; add eggs, bananas, and vanilla. Stir well. Combine flour, baking soda, salt, baking powder, cinnamon, and ginger. Add to creamed mixture. Mix well. Drop by heaping teaspoons onto greased baking sheet and bake 10 minutes. Sandwich together with icing when cool.

Icing:

1 egg white, beaten

2 tablespoons flour

2 tablespoons milk

1 teaspoon vanilla

1 cup powdered sugar

¾ cup shortening

1½ cups powdered sugar

Cream egg white, flour, milk, vanilla, and 1 cup powdered sugar. Add shortening and 1½ cups powdered sugar and stir until creamy.

Mrs. Melvin P. Weaver
Osseo, Michigan

Crunchy Fudge Sandwiches

1 (6 ounce) package (1 cup) butterscotch chips
½ cup peanut butter
4 cups crisp rice cereal
1 (6 ounce) package (1 cup) semisweet chocolate chips
½ cup sifted powdered sugar
2 tablespoons butter
1 tablespoon water

Melt butterscotch chips and peanut butter in heavy saucepan over low heat, stirring until blended. Stir in crisp rice cereal. Press half of mixture into buttered 8x8-inch pan. Chill. Set remainder aside. Stir chocolate chips, powdered sugar, butter, and water over hot water until chocolate melts. Spread over chilled mixture. Top with reserved mixture. Chill. Cut into 1½-inch squares.

Annie Miller
Cantril, Iowa

• • •

God is more interested in taking us through obstacles than in removing them.

• • •

Coconut Oatmeal Cookies

2 cups all-purpose flour

1 cup granulated sugar

1 teaspoon baking powder

1 teaspoon soda

½ teaspoon salt

1 cup brown sugar

1 cup shortening

2 eggs

½ teaspoon vanilla

1½ cups quick cooking oats

1 cup coconut, flaked

1 cup walnuts, chopped

½ cup granulated sugar

Preheat oven to 375 degrees. Sift together flour, sugar, baking powder, soda, and salt. Add brown sugar, shortening, eggs, and vanilla. Beat well. Stir in oats, coconut, and walnuts. Roll dough into small balls. Dip tops in granulated sugar. Place on ungreased baking sheet. Bake 12 to 14 minutes. Yield: about 5½ dozen

Mary Alice Kulp
Narvon, Pennsylvania

Classic Chocolate Chip Cookies

1 cup butter, softened
¼ cup granulated sugar
¾ cup brown sugar
1 teaspoon vanilla
1 (4 serving) package vanilla instant pudding
   (optional)
2 eggs
2¼ cups flour
1 teaspoon baking soda
2 to 3 tablespoons hot water
12 ounces chocolate chips
1 cup walnuts, chopped (optional)

Preheat oven to 375 degrees. Combine butter, sugars, vanilla, and pudding mix. Beat until smooth and creamy. Beat in eggs. Add flour. Dissolve soda in hot water and add until mixed in. Stir in chocolate chips and nuts. (Batter will be stiff.) Drop by teaspoon onto greased baking sheet and bake 9 to 9 ½ minutes or until brown.

Mrs. Jake Gingerich
Corydon, Iowa

Old-Fashioned Ginger Cookies

2 cups molasses

1 cup sugar

2 cups shortening

10 cups flour (½ pastry and ½ bread flour)

1 teaspoon salt

2 tablespoons soda

1 teaspoon ginger

1 teaspoon cinnamon

2 cups sour milk or buttermilk

1 egg, beaten

Preheat oven to 350 degrees. In saucepan heat molasses and sugar. Add shortening and stir until smooth. Remove from heat. Sift together flour, salt, soda, ginger, and cinnamon. Add alternately with sour milk. Stir until smooth dough forms. Work with hands 5 minutes. Chill. Roll ½ inch thick. Cut into shapes. Glaze cookies with beaten egg. Bake on greased baking sheet 20 to 25 minutes. Yield: 8 dozen

Ruth S. Martin
Selins Grove, Pennsylvania

Frozen Strawberry Pudding

1 (8 ounce) package cream cheese, softened
¾ cup white sugar
1 quart strawberries, sliced
1 (8 ounce) carton frozen whipped topping, thawed
3 cups miniature marshmallows

Mix softened cream cheese with sugar until smooth. Add strawberries and frozen whipped topping, thawed. Add marshmallows and freeze.

Dianna Yoder
Goshen, Indiana

*If your mind goes blank,
don't forget to turn
off the sound.*

Butter Pecan Ice Cream

I tablespoon margarine, melted
⅔ cup brown sugar
½ cup pecans, chopped
½ teaspoon maple flavoring
I (4 serving) package instant vanilla pudding
I (4 serving) package instant butterscotch pudding
I pint cream
Milk (enough to fill rest of freezer
after other ingredients are added)

Mix all ingredients except milk and put in I-gallon ice cream freezer. Fill rest of ice cream freezer with milk and freeze.

Jacob Schwartz
Portland, Indiana

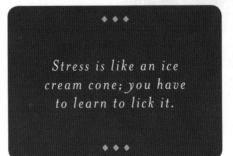

Stress is like an ice cream cone; you have to learn to lick it.

Homemade Fudgesicles

2 cups milk
1 (4 serving) package instant chocolate pudding
¼ cup sugar
1 cup evaporated milk or ¼ cup cream

Stir milk into pudding. Add sugar and evaporated milk or cream. Pour
into Popsicle containers and freeze.

Martha Yoder
Harrisville, Pennsylvania

Homemade Popsicles

2 (6 ounce) packages gelatin (any flavor)
2 cups sugar
2 packages Kool-Aid (any flavor)
4 cups boiling water
4 cups cold water

Combine all ingredients except cold water and mix well. Add cold water.
Pour into containers and freeze.

Mary Ann Yoder
Woodhull, New York

Ice Cream Jell-O

1 package flavored gelatin
Vanilla ice cream, softened

Fix your favorite flavored gelatin as directed, but instead of stirring in the amount of cold water called for in package directions, stir in that amount of vanilla ice cream. Let set.

Sarah B. Eicher
Geneva, Indiana

Ice Cream Pudding

1 gallon vanilla ice cream
2 packages chocolate sandwich cookies
1 (16 ounce) frozen whipped topping, thawed

Melt ice cream so you can stir it well. Grind cookies and add to ice cream. Mix in whipped topping. Pour into 11x15x1-inch baking pan. Freeze.

Leah Schwartz
Portland, Indiana

Frozen Mocha
Marble Loaf

4 cups chocolate sandwich cookies, finely crushed
    (about 44 cookies)
6 tablespoons butter or margarine, melted
2 (8 ounce) packages cream cheese, softened
2 (14 ounce) cans sweetened condensed milk
2 teaspoons vanilla
1 (16 ounce) container frozen whipped topping, thawed
4 tablespoons instant coffee
2 tablespoons hot water
1 cup chocolate syrup

Combine cookie crumbs and butter. Press into lightly greased 9x13-inch pan. Beat cream cheese until light. Add milk and vanilla. Mix well. Fold in whipped topping. Set aside half of mixture. Dissolve coffee in hot water and fold into remaining cream cheese mixture. Fold in chocolate syrup. Spoon half of chocolate mixture over crust and top with half of cream cheese mixture. Repeat layers. Swirl chocolate with knife, cover and freeze 6 hours or overnight.

Elizabeth Shrock
Jamestown, Pennsylvania

Ritz Cracker Pie

3 egg whites
1 cup sugar
1 teaspoon baking powder
1 cup pecans
24 Ritz crackers, broken into crumbs
1 teaspoon vanilla
1 cup cream, whipped stiff
¼ cup sugar

Preheat oven to 350 degrees. Beat egg whites until stiff, adding sugar gradually. Fold in baking powder, pecans, Ritz cracker crumbs, and vanilla. Bake in buttered pie pan 25 minutes. When cool top with whipped cream (cream that has been chilled and whipped until stiff and sugar added).

Hint: Pie is also good with vanilla or chocolate pudding made according to package directions and put on top of pie before adding whipped cream.

Rose Bontrager
Topeka, Indiana

◆ ◆ ◆

It isn't hard to make a
mountain out of a molehill;
just add a little dirt.

◆ ◆ ◆

Peanut Butter Pie

3 ounces cream cheese
½ cup peanut butter
1 cup powdered sugar
1 teaspoon vanilla
12 ounces frozen whipped topping, thawed
1 9-inch pastry shell, baked
¼ cup chocolate syrup

Mix cream cheese and peanut butter. Add powdered sugar, vanilla, and 8 ounces of whipped topping. Stir until blended. Put in baked pastry shell and top with remainder of whipped topping. Crisscross top of pie with chocolate syrup and top with peanut butter crumbs.

Peanut Butter Crumbs:
1 cup powdered sugar
⅓ cup peanut butter

Mix powdered sugar and peanut butter until crumbly.

Rose Bontrager
Topeka, Indiana

No-Sugar Sweet Yam Pie

4 yams, cooked and mashed
¼ cup honey
3 tablespoons butter
1 tablespoon cinnamon
½ teaspoon salt
½ cup orange juice
¼ cup maple syrup
3 egg yolks
½ teaspoon vanilla
3 egg whites
Pinch of cream of tartar
1 pastry shell, unbaked
¼ cup pecans, whole or chopped

Preheat oven to 325 degrees. Blend yams, honey, butter, cinnamon, salt, orange juice, maple syrup, egg yolks, and vanilla until smooth, using a potato masher. Beat egg whites and cream of tartar until peaks form. Fold into batter and pour into unbaked pastry shell. Bake 40 minutes or until set. Garnish with pecans.

Janine Merdian
Lacon, Illinois

Perfect Pumpkin Pie

I cup pumpkin or squash, cooked

1½ cups brown sugar

I teaspoon salt

½ teaspoon allspice

½ teaspoon cloves

I teaspoon cinnamon

4 tablespoons flour

4 egg yolks

4 cups milk

I teaspoon vanilla

4 egg whites, stiffly beaten

2 (9 inch) pastry shells, unbaked

Preheat oven to 375 degrees. Combine pumpkin, brown sugar, salt, allspice, cloves, cinnamon, flour, egg yolks, milk, and vanilla until well blended. Fold in egg whites that have been beaten until stiff. Pour into unbaked pastry shells. Bake I hour or until knife inserted into pie comes out clean.

Mrs. Harvey R. Miller
South Dayton, New York

Country Fair Pie

½ cup butter or margarine, melted

1 cup sugar

½ cup flour

2 eggs

1 teaspoon vanilla

1 cup (6 ounces) semi-sweet chocolate chips

1 cup nuts, chopped

½ cup butterscotch chips

1 (9 inch) unbaked pastry shell

In a mixing bowl, beat butter, sugar, flour, eggs, and vanilla until well blended. Stir in chips and nuts. Pour into unbaked pastry shell. Bake at 325 degrees for 1 hour or until golden brown. Cool on wire rack.

Susan Schwartz
Berne, Indiana

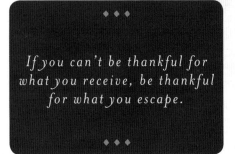

If you can't be thankful for what you receive, be thankful for what you escape.

Streusel-Top Fruit Pie

Pastry:

2 teaspoons sugar

1 teaspoon salt

½ cup cooking oil

2 tablespoons milk

1½ cups flour

Combine sugar, salt, oil, and milk. Add flour to form soft pastry dough. Press pastry into 9-inch pie pan. Flute if desired.

Fruit Filling:

½ cup powdered sugar

⅓ cup flour

4 cups sliced fresh peaches* or 2
        (1 pound, 13 ounce) cans drained sliced peaches

Combine in mixing bowl. Mix well. Spoon into unbaked crust.

Streusel Topping:

¾ cup flour

½ cup firmly packed brown sugar

½ teaspoon cinnamon

⅓ cup butter or margarine, softened

Preheat oven to 375 degrees. Combine flour, brown sugar, cinnamon, and butter to form crumb mixture. Spoon over peaches. Bake 40 to 45 minutes until topping is golden brown.

*Note: or substitute 4 cups fresh blueberries or fresh halved strawberries

Esther Borntrager
Beeville, Texas

Pineapple Philly Pie

1 (20 ounce) can pineapple pie filling
1 (8 ounce) package cream cheese, softened
½ cup sugar
½ teaspoon salt
2 eggs
½ cup milk
½ teaspoon vanilla
1 (9 inch) unbaked pastry shell

Preheat oven to 400 degrees. Spread pineapple filling over bottom of unbaked pastry shell. Beat cream cheese until soft and smooth. Slowly blend in sugar and salt. Add eggs one at a time, stirring well after each addition. Blend in milk and vanilla. Pour cream cheese mixture over pineapple. Bake 10 minutes. Reduce heat to 325 degrees for an additional 40 minutes. Cool before serving.

Mrs. John J. Byler
Middlefield, Ohio

♦ ♦ ♦

The one thing worse than a quitter is the person who is afraid to start.

♦ ♦ ♦

Apple Cream Pie

3 cups apples, finely chopped
1 cup brown sugar
¼ teaspoon salt
1 rounded tablespoon flour
1 cup cream
1 (9 inch) unbaked pastry shell

Preheat oven to 450 degrees. Mix apples, brown sugar, salt, flour, and cream. Put in unbaked pastry shell. Bake 15 minutes. Reduce heat to 325 degrees for an additional 30 to 40 minutes. When pie is about half done, take a knife and push top apples down to soften.

Mandy R. Schwartz
Portland, Indiana

*If you think you know
everything, you have
a lot to learn.*

Wonder Crunch Pie

3 eggs, slightly beaten
1 cup light corn syrup
1 cup white or brown sugar
⅓ teaspoon salt
¼ cup margarine, melted
1 teaspoon vanilla
½ cup coconut
½ cup pecan meal
1 (9 inch) unbaked pastry shell

Preheat oven to 450 degrees. Beat eggs, corn syrup, sugar, salt, margarine, and vanilla with rotary beater. Stir in coconut and pecan meal. Pour into unbaked pastry shell. Bake 10 minutes. Reduce heat to 350 degrees for an additional 30 to 40 minutes or until set.

Mary Bontrager
Kenton, Ohio

Kentucky Chocolate Chip Pie

1 stick margarine, melted

2 eggs, beaten

1 cup white sugar

1 teaspoon vanilla

1 cup chocolate chips

1 cup nuts, chopped

1 (9 inch) unbaked pastry shell

Preheat oven to 325 degrees. Melt margarine and set aside. Beat eggs, sugar, and vanilla. Add chocolate chips and nuts. Add margarine and beat well. Put in unbaked pastry shell. Bake 50 minutes or until done.

Alma D. Byler
Sommerfield, Ohio

French Rhubarb Pie

I egg, beaten
I cup sugar
2 rounded tablespoons flour
I teaspoon vanilla
2 cups rhubarb, diced
I (9 inch) unbaked pastry shell

Preheat oven to 400 degrees. Mix all ingredients and pour into unbaked pastry shell.

Topping:
¾ cup flour
½ cup brown sugar
⅓ cup margarine

Mix flour, sugar, and margarine. Sprinkle on top of rhubarb mixture. Bake 10 minutes. Reduce heat to 350 degrees for an additional 30 minutes or until done.

Mary Byler
Woodsfield, Ohio

Angel Cream Pie

1 cup half-and-half
1 cup heavy whipping cream
½ cup sugar
⅛ teaspoon salt
2 tablespoons (slightly rounded) flour
1 teaspoon vanilla
2 egg whites, stiffly beaten
1 (9 inch) unbaked pastry shell

Preheat oven to 350 degrees. In saucepan, combine half-and-half and whipping cream. Warm only slightly. Turn off heat and add, beating with whisk, sugar, salt, and flour. Add vanilla and fold in stiffly beaten egg whites. Pour into unbaked pastry shell. Bake 45 minutes or until just a little shaky.

Betty Miller
Goshen, Indiana

♦ ♦ ♦

Be like a postage stamp;
stick to one thing until
you get there.

♦ ♦ ♦

Sour Cream Peach Pie

1 egg, beaten
½ teaspoon salt
½ teaspoon vanilla
1 cup sour cream
¾ cup sugar
2 tablespoons flour
2½ cups fresh peaches, sliced
1 (9 inch) unbaked pastry shell

Topping:
½ cup butter
⅓ cup sugar
⅓ cup flour
1 teaspoon cinnamon

Preheat oven to 375 degrees. Combine egg, salt, vanilla, sour cream, sugar, and flour. Add peaches and stir. Pour into unbaked pastry shell and bake 30 minutes or until pie is slightly brown. Remove pie from oven. Combine topping ingredients, spread on top of pie, and bake 15 minutes longer.

Sylvia Miller
Rossiter, Pennsylvania

Drumstick Pudding

Crust:
1½ cups graham cracker crumbs
¼ cup margarine, melted
¼ cup sugar

Mix graham cracker crumbs, margarine, and sugar. Press on bottom of 9x13-inch pan.

Filling:
2 (8 ounce) packages cream cheese, softened
1 (16 ounce) carton frozen whipped topping, thawed
1 cup powdered sugar
¼ cup peanut butter
1 (6 serving) package instant chocolate pudding
1 (4 serving) package instant vanilla pudding
5 cups milk

Mix cream cheese, whipped topping, powdered sugar, and peanut butter and spread over crust. Prepare pudding mixes according to package directions. Layer chocolate and vanilla on top of cream cheese mixture.

Optional: Put chopped nuts on top. Tastes like a Drumstick ice cream cone.

Ella Detweiler
Atlantic, Pennsylvania

Date Pudding

Cake:

1 cup dates, finely chopped

1 teaspoon baking soda

1 cup hot water

1 cup brown sugar

1 tablespoon butter

1 cup flour

1 egg

½ cup nuts

Mix dates, soda, and water and let set until cool. Add brown sugar, butter, flour, egg, and nuts. Stir. Preheat oven to 350 degrees. Pour into greased baking pan. Bake 20 to 30 minutes.

Sauce:

2 tablespoons butter

1 cup brown sugar

1½ cups water

3 tablespoons ClearJel (or 2 tablespoons cornstarch)

2 teaspoons vanilla

1½ teaspoons maple flavoring

2 tablespoons maple pancake syrup

Layers:

1 (8 ounce) carton frozen whipped topping, thawed

2 to 3 bananas

Boil butter, brown sugar, water, and ClearJel 10 minutes. Add vanilla, maple flavoring, and syrup. When ready to serve, alternate layers of cake, sauce, whipped topping, and bananas.

Mrs. Harvey R. Miller
South Dayton, New York

Oreo Pudding

First Layer:
Crush 1-pound package Oreo cookies to form crust.

Reserve some crumbs for topping. Layer on bottom of 9x13-inch pan.

Second Layer:
1 (8 ounce) package cream cheese, softened
1 cup powdered sugar
1½ cups frozen whipped topping, thawed

Mix cream cheese and powdered sugar. Add whipped topping. Layer on top of crust.

Third Layer:
1 (6 serving) package instant chocolate pudding. Mix as directed.

Layer on top of cream cheese mixture.

Fourth Layer:
1 (8 ounce) carton frozen whipped topping, thawed
Oreo cookie crumbs reserved from crust.

Layer whipped topping on pudding and sprinkle with reserved crushed Oreo cookies. Chill.

Joanna Miller
Hersey, Michigan

Cherry O' Cream Cheese Pudding

Graham Cracker Crust:

1½ cups graham cracker crumbs

¼ cup margarine, melted

¼ cup sugar

Mix graham cracker crumbs, margarine, and sugar. Press into bottom of 9x13-inch pan.

Filling:

1 (14 ounce) can sweetened condensed milk

1 (8 ounce) package cream cheese, softened

⅓ cup lemon juice

1 teaspoon vanilla

2 (20 ounce) cans cherry pie filling

1 (8 ounce) carton frozen whipped topping, thawed

Combine condensed milk and cream cheese. Add lemon juice and vanilla. Pour over graham cracker crust. Pour cherry pie filling over cream cheese mixture. Spread with whipped topping if desired. Chill.

Esther A. Hershberger
Goshen, Indiana

Cinnamon Pudding

4 tablespoons margarine

4 cups brown sugar

4 cups water

2 cups sugar

4 tablespoons margarine

4 teaspoons baking powder

4 teaspoons cinnamon

4 teaspoons vanilla

2¼ cups milk

¾ cup nuts, chopped

Preheat oven to 350 degrees. In saucepan, combine 4 tablespoons margarine, brown sugar, and water and bring to a boil. Meanwhile, combine sugar, 4 tablespoons margarine, baking powder, cinnamon, vanilla, and milk and mix well. Put into a greased 9x13-inch pan and pour boiling sugar mixture over top. Bake 10 minutes. Sprinkle nuts over top of pudding and bake 10 minutes more. Delicious served with whipped topping or ice cream. Serve warm.

Anna Stutzman
Arcola, Illinois

• • •

*God judges us by what
we do, not by what
others say.*

• • •

Caramel Pudding

I stick margarine (½ cup)
2 cups brown sugar
Pinch of soda
3 quarts milk
I to I½ cups ClearJel or I cup cornstarch
I teaspoon vanilla
Pinch of salt

Melt margarine and brown sugar in heavy saucepan, stirring constantly until browned. Stir in soda and add milk. Heat until hot, then thicken with ClearJel. Add vanilla and salt. (If you prefer it sweeter, use less milk.)

Marion Stauffer
Mechanicsville, Maryland

Coffee Pudding

3 teaspoons instant coffee
½ cup warm water
1 (14 ounce) can sweetened condensed milk
1 (4 serving) package instant vanilla pudding
1½ cups water
1 cup frozen whipped topping, thawed

Dissolve coffee in ½ cup warm water. Add milk, pudding mix, water, and whipped topping. Beat. Let set before serving.

Janet M. Martin
Ephrata, Pennsylvania

◆ ◆ ◆

A happy home is not merely having a roof over your head; it's having a foundation under your feet.

◆ ◆ ◆

Simple Caramel Krispy Rolls

2 cups brown sugar
1 (14 ounce) can sweetened condensed milk
1 cup light corn syrup
1 cup butter

In saucepan, combine brown sugar, milk, syrup, and butter and boil 12 minutes, stirring constantly. Let cool.

While cooling, mix:
½ cup butter, melted over low heat
8 cups miniature marshmallows
10 cups crisp rice cereal

Melt butter. Add marshmallows and melt, stirring constantly. Add crisp rice cereal and mix well. Spread to ½ inch thick on large buttered baking sheets. Spread caramel mixture on top, roll up like a jelly roll, and slice.

Saloma Stutzman
Navarre, Ohio

Granny Smith Apple Dessert

1 Granny Smith apple
1 tube crescent rolls
1 stick butter
1 cup brown sugar
1 cup Mountain Dew

Preheat oven to 350 degrees. Peel and core apple. Slice into 8 slices.
Microwave slices 2 minutes on paper towel or bake in 250-degree oven
5 to 6 minutes. Wrap each apple slice in a crescent roll and place in
8x8-inch pan. Melt butter and brown sugar. Do not boil. Pour over rolls.
Then pour 1 cup of Mountain Dew over the mixture. Bake 50 minutes or
until golden brown and set.

Ida Marchand
Goshen, Indiana

*The glory of tomorrow
is rooted in the drudgery
of today.*

Pineapple Rings

1 can (14 ounce) sweetened condensed milk
1 can pineapple slices (10 slices)
Frozen whipped topping, thawed
Maraschino cherries (optional)

Cook unopened can of sweetened condensed milk 3 hours in kettle of water. Make sure water covers can at all times. Then refrigerate can until cold. Spread pineapple slices out on a plate. Open both ends of milk can with a can opener. Remove one end and use the other to push up the thickened milk. Cut the milk into 10 slices as you push up from the bottom. Top each pineapple slice with a milk slice. Then top each with a dab of whipped topping and garnish with a maraschino cherry.

(Hint: Dip your knife blade in boiling water between every cut through the milk. It will cut a lot easier.)

Dianna Yoder
Goshen, Indiana

*You can give without loving,
but you can't love
without giving.*

Broken Glass Dessert

24 graham crackers (crushed)
½ cup brown sugar
¼ cup butter, melted
3 small boxes flavored gelatin (assorted flavors)
2 cups whipped topping
1 (8 ounce) package cream cheese, softened
½ cup white sugar
1 teaspoon vanilla
1 cup crushed pineapple, drained

Mix crackers, brown sugar, and butter. Spread in bottom of glass 9x13-inch pan or bowl. Reserve some crumbs to sprinkle on top. Dissolve each package of flavored gelatin in ½ cup boiling water. Chill gelatin in separate pans. Cut into cubes. Beat whipped topping, cream cheese, sugar, and vanilla. Fold in pineapple and gelatin cubes. Pour on top of crumb crust. Sprinkle with remaining crumbs. Chill.

Maria Schrock
Princeton, Missouri

Blueberry Cream Cheese Squares

¼ cup cornstarch

½ cup sugar

½ cup water

⅓ cup blueberries (drained)

2 cups graham cracker crumbs

1½ sticks butter, melted

1½ cups sugar

2 teaspoons vanilla

2 (8 ounce) packages cream cheese, softened

1 package Dream Whip or ¾ cup cream, whipped

Combine cornstarch, sugar, water, and blueberries. Cook until thick. Cool. Combine graham cracker crumbs and melted butter. Press two-thirds of crumbs in bottom of 9x13-inch pan, saving remaining crumbs for the top. Beat sugar and vanilla into cream cheese. Fold in whipped topping. Spread half cream cheese mixture over crumbs. Spread blueberry filling over cheese layer. Layer remaining cheese mixture over blueberries and top with remaining crumbs. Chill.

Note: You may substitute raspberries or cherries for the blueberries.

Ida C. Miller
Medford, Wisconsin

Strawberry Pizza

½ cup margarine

¾ cup sugar

1 egg

1⅓ cup flour

¼ teaspoon salt

1 teaspoon baking powder

1 (8 ounce) package cream cheese, softened

½ cup sugar

1 (8 ounce) carton frozen whipped topping, thawed

1½ quarts strawberries

1 package strawberry glaze

Preheat oven to 375 degrees. Cream margarine, sugar, and egg. Add flour, salt, and baking powder. Spread on pizza pan and bake 10 minutes. In mixing bowl, combine cream cheese, remaining ½ cup sugar, and whipped topping. Spread over cooled crust. Combine strawberries and glaze mixture and spread over top. Refrigerate to set.

Mrs. Paul H. Schwartz Sr.
Fremont, Michigan

The dictionary is the only place where success comes before work.

Cottage Cheese Dessert

8 ounces crushed pineapple, drained (save juice)
3 ounces flavored gelatin
12 ounces cottage cheese
12 ounces frozen whipped topping, thawed

Stir dry gelatin into pineapple juice. Mix cottage cheese and whipped topping. Add pineapple and gelatin. Chill.

Mrs. Norman L. Miller
Clark, Missouri

Scotcharoos

1 cup sugar
1 cup light corn syrup
1 cup peanut butter
6 cups crisp rice cereal
1 cup chocolate chips
1 cup butterscotch chips

In large saucepan, mix sugar and corn syrup. Bring to a very slight boil. Remove from heat and add peanut butter and crisp rice cereal. Mix thoroughly. Press into bottom of greased 9x13-inch pan. In double boiler, melt chocolate and butterscotch chips and spread over top of crisp rice cereal.

Linda Stoltzfus
Orrstown, Pennsylvania

Elkhart and LaGrange Counties, Indiana

In 1841 four Amish families moved from Pennsylvania to northern Indiana. Now there are more than 20,000 Amish living in Elkhart and LaGrange counties, making them the third largest population of Amish in America.

The black soil in these counties is fertile. Some Amish men living in this area grow corn, soybeans, oats, hay, barley, and rye, either as a full-time living or to supplement their income. Many others work in nearby factories and stores. Some have workshops of their own, and there are numerous home-based businesses in the area, such as bulk-food stores, furniture shops, quilt shops, cheese stores, variety stores, and bicycle shops, that support Amish families.

A large flea market is held in Shipshewana, Indiana, every year, opening in May. The flea market brings in many English and Amish people who come to buy and sell their wares. There are also plenty of auctions held in the area, including horse auctions, such as the one in Topeka.

The Old Order Amish living in Elkhart and LaGrange counties drive black buggies in various sizes. Many of the Amish ride bicycles and can often be seen pulling small carts used to haul supplies and things they might buy on a shopping trip to town.

Maple Lane Wildlife Farm in Topeka is sometimes referred to as the "Amish Zoo." The Amish owners of the farm raise bears, camels, and many other animals one might find in a zoo.

The Amish in northern Indiana strive to maintain their heritage. They value hard work, simplicity, and a closeness to God, as well as to their families.

Jams and Jellies

And he said, My presence shall go with thee, and I will give thee rest.

EXODUS 33:14

Elderberry Jelly

3 cups elderberry juice
4½ cups sugar—no substitute
1 box Sure-Jell—not pectin

- Measure exact amount of juice into 6-quart saucepan.
- Do not make more than one recipe at a time.
- Measure exact amount of sugar into a separate bowl. Set aside. Do not reduce sugar or use a sugar substitute.
- Pour Sure-Jell into fruit juice, stirring constantly. Bring mixture to a full rolling boil (a boil that doesn't stop bubbling when being stirred, on high heat).
- Stir in sugar quickly. Return to full boil, stirring constantly. Boil 1 minute only.
- Remove from heat. Quickly ladle into prepared jars.
- Tighten lids and turn jars upside down for 10 minutes. Then turn jars right side up to cool and seal.
- Let jelly jars stand at room temperature for 24 hours.
- Makes about 5 cups.

To Remake Thin Jelly That Doesn't Set Up

Put 1 cup cold water and 1 box Sure-Jell in pan and stir constantly. Boil 2 minutes and set aside. In another saucepan, add 22 tablespoons sugar into the thin jelly (needing to be recooked). Stir constantly. When it starts to boil, add Sure-Jell and water mixture. Boil at a full rolling boil 1 minute. Put in jars according to above directions.

Mary and Katie Yoder
Goshen, Indiana

Rhubarb Jelly

5 cups rhubarb, cut up
½ cup water
4 cups sugar
1 large box strawberry gelatin

Combine rhubarb, water, and sugar. Boil 5 minutes. Remove from heat and stir in strawberry gelatin until dissolved. Pour into jars and seal with paraffin.

Amanda Schwartz
Monroe, Indiana

Peach Jelly

12 cups peaches, ground
5 cups sugar
1½ cups orange gelatin

Cook peaches and sugar 20 minutes. Stir in gelatin until dissolved. Pour into jars and seal.

Mrs. Joseph Zook
Rebersburg, Pennsylvania

Low-Sugar Strawberry Freezer Jam

¾ cup ClearJel
6 cups sugar
6 cups strawberries, mashed
3 packages (1 cup) Sure-Jell
2¼ cups water

Mix ClearJel with 1 cup sugar. Add rest of sugar to strawberries and let set 15 minutes. Mix Sure-Jell with 2¼ cups water and boil 1 minute. Pour over strawberries and stir well. Add ClearJel mixture and beat 3 minutes. Pour into containers and let stand 24 hours at room temperature before freezing.

This recipe can also be used for peach jam. Note: If weather is very warm, let containers set out not more than 12 hours before freezing.

Ruth Ann Zimmerman
Elma, Iowa

◆ ◆ ◆

Unless you put out your water jars when it rains, you won't catch any water.

◆ ◆ ◆

Zucchini Jelly

6 cups zucchini, peeled and grated
6 cups sugar
2 tablespoons lemon juice
8 ounces crushed pineapple and juice
6 ounces apricot, peach, or orange gelatin

In heavy saucepan, cook zucchini 6 minutes. Add sugar, lemon juice, and pineapple and cook 6 minutes more. Then add 6 ounces gelatin and stir until dissolved. Put in jars to seal or freeze.

Lydia Bontrager
Kenton, Ohio

Rhubarb Preserves

8 cups rhubarb, chopped
8 cups sugar
2 (20 ounce) cans crushed pineapple
12 ounces raspberry gelatin

Combine rhubarb and sugar and let set 2½ hours or overnight. In heavy saucepan, cook rhubarb mixture 10 minutes. Add crushed pineapple and cook for another 10 minutes. Add gelatin and stir until dissolved. Put in jars and seal.

Mrs. Daniel J. Bontrager
Kenton, Ohio

Pepper Butter

40 hot peppers, ground
6 cups sugar
1 quart vinegar
3 cups yellow mustard
1 tablespoon salt
1¼ cups flour
1¼ cups water

Grind peppers and mix with sugar, vinegar, mustard, and salt. Boil 10 to 15 minutes. Mix flour and water and slowly add to pepper mixture. Cook 5 more minutes, stirring constantly. Pour into jars and seal. Delicious on BLT sandwiches and other sandwiches.
Yield: 8½ pints

Rebecca Lambright
Scottville, Michigan

Webster County, Missouri

Since 1968 Old Order Amish have lived in Webster County, Missouri, twenty-six miles east of Springfield, and not far from Seymour. Many of these Amish originally came from Berne, Indiana. Since they are of Swiss-German descent, they are often referred to as the "yodeling Amish," because they like to yodel much like the natives of the Swiss Alps.

The Amish in Webster County are a lot plainer that most other Amish communities in Missouri. They drive black buggies with no tops, no enclosed cabs, and no rubber tires. When they must travel out of the area, they hire English drivers.

The Webster County Amish have their own one-room schoolhouses, which their children attend until eighth grade. Young people play softball, basketball, and other outdoor games, and the young men are strong wrestlers.

There are several Amish-run stores and shops near Seymour, but since this small community is not on a main road, one has to seek out their places of business. The Amish living in the area are very frugal, and like most other Amish, do not allow electricity or phones in their homes. The Amish of Webster County are friendly people and make good neighbors and helpful friends.

# Main Dishes

And now abideth faith, hope, charity,
these three; but the greatest of these is charity.

1 Corinthians 13:13

Poppy Seed Chicken

4 cups chicken breast, chopped in small pieces,
    cooked or uncooked
1 can cream of chicken soup
1 can cream of celery soup
1 cup sour cream
1 tablespoon poppy seeds
1 stick butter
1 sleeve Ritz Crackers, crushed

Preheat oven to 350 degrees. Mix chicken with soups, sour cream, and poppy seeds and pour into greased 9x13-inch baking dish. Melt butter in skillet and sauté crushed crackers until browned. Sprinkle crackers over top of chicken mixture and bake 30 minutes. Serve over rice or noodles.

Rachel Yoder
Topeka, Indiana

♦ ♦ ♦

Happiness is not found in the abundance of things we possess, but as we work and share for the welfare of others, our need for many possessions grows less.

♦ ♦ ♦

Chickenetti

6 ounces spaghetti noodles, cooked

2 cups chicken, cooked and diced

1 (10½ ounce) can cream of mushroom soup

2 cups corn

½ cup chicken broth

⅛ teaspoon celery salt

1 teaspoon salt

¼ teaspoon pepper

¾ pound Velveeta, shredded

Preheat oven to 300 degrees. Mix all ingredients and put in casserole dish. Bake covered 1 hour.

Mary Newswanger
Shippensburg, Pennsylvania

Poor Man's Steak

3 pounds ground beef
1 cup saltine cracker crumbs
1 cup water
¼ cup onions, chopped
Salt and pepper to taste
1 cup flour
1 can cream of mushroom soup
¼ to ½ cup milk
1 to 2 teaspoons Gravy Master (or Kitchen Bouquet)

Mix ground beef, cracker crumbs, water, onions, salt, and pepper and press in a baking sheet. Chill overnight to set.

When ready to bake, preheat oven to 350 degrees. Cut ground beef mixture in squares, roll in flour, and fry on both sides. Place in baking dish. Combine soup, milk, and Gravy Master and pour over meat. Bake 1 hour.

Mrs. Reuben Byler
Woodsfield, Ohio

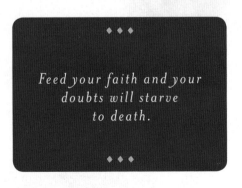

*Feed your faith and your
doubts will starve
to death.*

Beef Volcanoes

1½ pounds ground beef

2 eggs

¾ cup tomato juice

1½ cups oatmeal

1 teaspoon dry mustard

1 tablespoon Worcestershire sauce

1½ teaspoons salt

¼ teaspoon pepper

10 (1-inch) squares Velveeta

1 cup tomato juice

Preheat oven to 350 degrees. Combine beef, eggs, ¾ cup tomato juice, oatmeal, mustard, Worcestershire sauce, salt, and pepper. Mix well. Shape into balls and press Velveeta into center. Place balls in greased casserole and pour 1 cup tomato juice over top. Bake 35 to 40 minutes.

Rosanna Zimmerman
New Holland, Pennsylvania

Popover Pizza

1 pound ground beef

1 small onion, chopped

1 pint pizza sauce

Cheese, shredded, any kind and amount desired

2 eggs

1 tablespoon vegetable oil

1 cup milk

1 cup dry baking mix

Preheat oven to 350 degrees. Lightly grease 9x13-inch pan. First layer:
Fry ground beef with onion. Add pizza sauce and layer in bottom of pan.
Second layer: Sprinkle with cheese. Third layer: Stir together eggs, oil,
milk, and baking mix. Pour over top and bake 30 minutes.

Mrs. Amos Yoder
Marlette, Michigan

When we are willing to do what we can, we will be surprised at how much we can do.

Wiggles

2 (1 pound) packages spaghetti, broken up

9 slices bacon

3 pounds ground beef

3 medium onions

3 cups carrots, sliced

3 cups celery, sliced

2 cups peas

2 cans cream of mushroom soup

3 teaspoons salt

1 pound Velveeta, shredded

1½ to 2 pints tomato soup

Cook spaghetti according to package directions. Fry bacon and remove from skillet. Cook ground beef and onions in bacon grease. Put cooked meat into roaster. Add carrots, celery, peas, mushroom soup, salt, and spaghetti. Arrange bacon on spaghetti. Add cheese. Pour tomato soup over top and bake 1½ to 2 hours. Yield: a large roaster full

Frances Wengerd
Loyal, Wisconsin

BBQ Beef Sandwiches

2 medium onions, chopped
1 cup celery, chopped
¼ cup butter
1½ cups sugar
4 teaspoons prepared mustard
¼ teaspoon pepper
1 tablespoon lemon juice
1 cup chili sauce
2 tablespoons Worcestershire sauce
Salt to taste
4 cups cooked beef, shredded
12 to 15 buns

Sauté onions and celery in butter until tender. Add sugar, mustard, pepper, lemon juice, chili sauce, Worcestershire sauce, and salt. Simmer 20 minutes. Add beef and heat thoroughly. Spoon onto buns. Serves approximately 12 to 15.

Mrs. Kevin Nolt
Willard, Ohio

Bacon-Wrapped Chicken

6 chicken breasts, skinned and boneless
1 (8 ounce) carton cream cheese with onion and chives, whipped
1 tablespoon butter
Salt to taste
6 bacon strips

Preheat oven to 400 degrees. Flatten chicken breasts to ½ inch thickness. Spread 3 tablespoons cream cheese over each. Dot each with butter and sprinkle with salt. Roll up and wrap each with a strip of bacon. Place seam down in a greased 9x13-inch baking dish. Bake uncovered 35 to 45 minutes or until juice runs clear. Broil 6 inches from heat 5 minutes or until bacon is crisp.

Annie Jean Smucker
Quarryville, Pennsylvania

Baked Hamburgers

1 pound ground beef
½ cup milk
½ cup bread crumbs
2 eggs
¾ teaspoon salt
Tomato juice

Preheat oven to 350 degrees. Combine ground beef, milk, bread crumbs, eggs, salt, and enough tomato juice so mixture will stick together. Make into patties, brown in skillet, then put into casserole dish. (Patties can also be put on baking sheet and baked in oven.)

Sauce:
½ cup water
2 teaspoons mustard
2 teaspoons vinegar
1 cup celery, chopped
½ cup ketchup
½ cup sugar
1 medium onion, chopped
½ teaspoon salt

Combine all ingredients and pour sauce over patties. Bake 1 hour.

Rachel C. Peachey
Jackson, Ohio

First-Course Pie

3 cups potatoes, shredded
3 teaspoons vegetable oil
1 pint sausage
1 pint peas
1 cup cheese, shredded
1 cup milk
2 eggs, beaten
½ teaspoon salt
⅛ teaspoon pepper

Preheat oven to 425 degrees. Mix potatoes and oil. Press into pie plate. Bake 15 minutes or until crust begins to brown. Remove from oven and layer on sausage, peas, and cheese. Mix milk, eggs, salt, and pepper and pour over top. Bake 1 hour longer in 375-degree oven or until lightly browned and set. Cool 5 minutes before serving.

Mrs. Marion Stauffer
Mechanicsville, Maryland

* * *

The easiest way to finish a difficult job is to get to work. After the start is made, the finish is near at hand.

* * *

Green Rice

1¼ cups rice
1 teaspoon salt
4 cups water
3 poblano peppers (very mild chili pepper)
¾ stick butter, melted
2 cups sour cream
1½ pounds mozzarella/cheddar cheese, shredded, divided
3 cups chicken, cooked and chopped

Preheat oven to 350 degrees. Cook rice in salted water. Cook peppers and remove stems. Blend peppers, butter, sour cream, and ½ pound cheese in a blender or with a rotary beater. Pour over rice and chicken and mix well. Pour into greased 9x13-inch pan and top with rest of cheese. Bake 20 to 30 minutes or until heated. Serve on warm tortilla shells topped with salsa and sour cream or ranch dressing.

Lila Yoder
Montezuma, GA

To ease another's burden, we need to help to carry it.

Home-Style Scalloped Potatoes

⅓ cup onions, chopped
5 tablespoons butter or margarine
5 tablespoons flour
1¼ teaspoons salt
½ teaspoon pepper
5 cups milk
6 cups potatoes, thinly sliced

Preheat oven to 350 degrees. In large saucepan, sauté onion in butter until tender. Stir in flour, salt, and pepper. Gradually add milk. Bring to a boil and cook and stir 2 minutes or until sauce is thickened. Place half of potatoes in greased 3-quart baking dish. Pour half of sauce over potatoes. Repeat layers. Bake uncovered 60 to 70 minutes or until potatoes are tender and top is lightly browned.

Linda Peachey
Beaver, Ohio

Crispy Baked Potatoes

6 medium potatoes
⅓ cup melted margarine or butter
I teaspoon salt
I cup crushed cornflakes

Wash and peel potatoes. Cut each into 4 wedges. Dip wedges in margarine or butter and sprinkle with salt. Roll in cereal crumbs. Place in greased baking dish and bake at 400 degrees for 40 minutes.

Sarah Troyer
Mercer, Pennsylvania

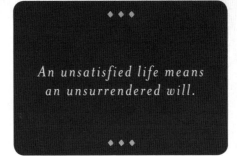

*An unsatisfied life means
an unsurrendered will.*

Goulash

1 cup elbow macaroni
Boiling water
1 pound ground beef
1 medium onion, chopped
2 cups celery, chopped
1 (2 ounce) can mushrooms, undrained
1 green pepper, chopped
1 (15 ounce) can tomato sauce or 3 cups tomato juice
½ cup ketchup
1 teaspoon salt
¼ teaspoon pepper
1 cup water

Place macaroni in small bowl. Cover with boiling water; let set. While macaroni blanches, cook ground beef and onion in heavy saucepan. Drain fat. Drain macaroni and add to meat along with celery, mushrooms, pepper, tomato sauce, ketchup, seasonings, and water. Mix thoroughly. Cover and simmer 30 minutes, stirring occasionally.

Edna D. Stutzman
Clare, Michigan

Chicken Curry

3 tablespoons margarine

¼ cup onion, chopped

1½ teaspoons curry powder

3 tablespoons flour

⅛ teaspoon ground ginger

¾ teaspoon salt

¾ teaspoon sugar

1 cup chicken broth

1 cup milk

2 cups chicken, cooked and cubed

Cooked rice

Melt margarine and sauté onion and curry powder. Blend in flour, ginger, salt, and sugar. Stir in broth and milk. Bring to a boil, stirring constantly for 1 minute. Add chicken and heat through. Serve over rice.

Mrs. Terrence Wenger
Elkhorn, Kentucky

Savory Meat Loaf

2 pounds ground beef
¼ cup onions, chopped
1 cup oatmeal
1 egg
2½ teaspoons salt
¼ teaspoon pepper
1 teaspoon mustard
¼ cup ketchup
1 cup tomato juice
3 bacon slices

Preheat oven to 350 degrees. Combine beef, onions, oatmeal, egg, salt, pepper, mustard, ketchup, and tomato juice. Mix well. Put mixture into greased loaf pan and cover with bacon slices. Bake 45 minutes. Spread with glaze and bake 15 minutes longer or until done.

Glaze:
½ cup brown sugar
1½ teaspoons mustard
1 tablespoon Worcestershire sauce
Vinegar, enough to make a thick paste

Combine all ingredients.

Mrs. Melvin P. Weaver
Osseo, Michigan

Baked Ranch Chicken Breast

1 (1 ounce) packet Hidden Valley Ranch Mix
2 cups bread crumbs
6 to 8 pieces chicken breast
1 stick margarine, melted

Preheat oven to 350 degrees. Combine ranch dressing mix and bread crumbs. Dip chicken breasts in melted margarine and then in bread crumb mix. Bake on foil-lined baking sheet uncovered 30 minutes.

Mrs. David W. Byler
Summerfield, Ohio

Sausage and Rice Casserole

1 pound sausage
1 onion, chopped
1 can cream of chicken soup
1 can water
1 cup rice (Minute) or other rice, cooked
1 cup cheese, shredded

Preheat oven to 350 degrees. Brown sausage and onion. Drain fat. Add soup, water, rice, and cheese. Mix well. Put into greased casserole dish and bake 25 minutes.

Charlene Wenger
Elkhorn, Kentucky

Souper Meat 'n Potatoes Pie

1 can cream of mushroom soup

1 pound ground beef

¼ cup onion, finely chopped

1 egg, slightly beaten

¼ cup fine dry bread crumbs

2 tablespoons parsley, chopped

¼ teaspoon salt

Dash of pepper

2 cups mashed potatoes

¼ cup mild cheese, shredded

Preheat oven to 350 degrees. Mix thoroughly ½ cup soup, beef, onion, egg, bread crumbs, parsley, salt, and pepper. Press firmly into 9-inch pie plate. Bake 25 minutes. Spoon off fat. Frost with potatoes and top with remaining soup and cheese. Bake 10 minutes longer or until done. Garnish with cooked sliced bacon if desired.

Mary Mast
Amelia, Virginia

Beef and Noodle Casserole

1½ pounds ground beef

1 tablespoon butter or margarine

1 large onion, chopped

1 cup green pepper, chopped

1 tablespoon Worcestershire sauce

1 (10 ounce) package wide noodles cooked and drained

2 (10¾ ounce) cans cream of tomato soup

1 (10¾ ounce) can cream of mushroom soup

1 cup (4 ounces) cheddar cheese, shredded

Preheat oven to 350 degrees. Brown beef in large skillet. Remove beef and drain fat. In same skillet, melt butter over medium-high heat. Sauté onion and pepper until tender. Add beef, Worcestershire sauce, noodles, and soups. Mix well. Spoon into greased 3-quart casserole and top with cheese. Bake 45 minutes. Yield: 8 servings

Judith Martin
Millmont, Pennsylvania

Chicken Patties

3 cups chicken, cooked and shredded

½ cup mayonnaise

2 tablespoons lemon juice

½ cup onion, minced

½ teaspoon salt

¾ cup cracker crumbs

Combine chicken, mayonnaise, lemon juice, onion, and salt. Make into 8 patties. Dip into cracker crumbs and fry on both sides until golden brown. Good served with slaw.

Darlene Stauffer
Elkhorn, Kentucky

♦ ♦ ♦

We should be like a watch:
open face, busy hands,
pure gold, well-regulated,
and full of good works.

♦ ♦ ♦

Cowboy Hash

2 pounds ground beef
1 cup pork and beans
1 cup ketchup
4 cups mixed vegetables, cut up
4 tablespoons mustard
¼ cup brown sugar

Brown beef. Stir in pork and beans, ketchup, vegetables, mustard, and brown sugar. Heat thoroughly or until vegetables are done. Serve with corn bread.

Jacob Schwartz
Portland, Indiana

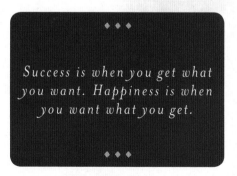

Success is when you get what you want. Happiness is when you want what you get.

Stuffed Peppers

1 pound ground beef
¼ cup onion, chopped
1½ cups whole kernel corn
1 (8 ounce) can tomato sauce
1 cup rice, cooked
¼ cup A 1 Steak Sauce
Black pepper to taste
6 large green peppers

Preheat oven to 350 degrees. Brown meat in skillet and pour off fat. Stir in corn, onion, tomato sauce, rice, steak sauce, and pepper. Set aside. Cut off tops of green peppers and remove seeds. Spoon meat mixture into peppers and arrange in baking pan. Bake 30 to 35 minutes. Makes 6 servings.

Ida B. Miller
Smicksburg, Pennsylvania

Wiener Stew

6 cups potatoes, diced

3 cups carrots, diced

2 onions, chopped

2 cups celery, diced

2 teaspoons salt

3 pints water

1 pound sliced wieners

2 tablespoons butter

¼ teaspoon pepper

2 tablespoons flour

1 cup milk

Cook potatoes, carrots, onions, and celery in salt water until soft. Add wieners, butter, and pepper. Bring to a boil. Thicken soup with flour and milk that have been shaken together to form a smooth paste. Yield: 8 servings

Regina Schlabach
Monticello, Kentucky

Ham and Bean Soup

¼ cup margarine
4 tablespoons flour
2 cans soup beans
½ cup milk
1½ cups ham bits
Water
Salt to taste

In heavy saucepan, heat and stir margarine and flour until golden brown. Add beans and milk. Mix. In skillet, brown ham bits and add enough water to make brown broth. Add ham and broth to beans and salt to taste. Simmer 15 minutes.

Sam Schwartz
Portland, Indiana

Stuffed Green Pepper Soup

½ cup green peppers, chopped

1 pound ground beef, browned

¼ teaspoon salt

⅛ teaspoon pepper

2 tablespoons Parmesan cheese

1 pint tomato juice

⅔ cup rice, cooked

⅛ to ¼ cup brown sugar

Combine all ingredients in large saucepan and cook until peppers are done.

Wilma Yoder
Dundee, Ohio

Chili Soup

2 pounds ground beef

1 large onion, chopped

2 quarts tomato juice or part water

1 quart kidney beans, cooked

½ cup pickle relish

1 tablespoon chili powder

½ cup brown sugar

2 tablespoons taco seasoning

Salt (to taste)

Black pepper (to taste)

Red pepper, dried (to taste)

⅓ cup ClearJel (or ¼ cup cornstarch)

1 tablespoon sugar

1 cup water

In skillet, brown ground beef and onion. Drain fat. In large pot, bring to boil tomato juice, kidney beans, relish, chili powder, brown sugar, taco seasoning, salt, black pepper, and red pepper. In separate bowl, mix ClearJel, sugar, and water. Add to tomato juice mixture. Stir constantly. Add ground beef mixture and cook until heated.

Freda Yoder
Goshen, Indiana

Hearty Hamburger Soup

2 tablespoons butter
1 pound ground beef
1 cup onion, chopped
2 cups tomato juice
1 cup carrots, sliced
½ cup peppers, chopped
1 cup potatoes, diced
1½ teaspoons salt
¼ teaspoon pepper
1 teaspoon seasoned salt
¼ cup flour
4 cups milk

Melt butter in saucepan and brown meat. Add onion and cook until transparent. Stir in tomato juice, carrots, peppers, potatoes, salt, pepper, and seasoned salt. Cover and cook over low heat until vegetables are tender, about 20 to 25 minutes. Combine flour with 1 cup milk and stir into soup mixture. Bring to a boil. Add remaining milk and heat through.

Betty Yoder
Rexford, Montana

Christian County, Kentucky

In 1989 the first Amish family moved from their home in Lancaster County, Pennsylvania, to Christian County, Kentucky, where they settled because land was cheaper and more abundant. A short time later, two more Amish families joined them. Since that time, many more Amish families have migrated to Christian County, as well as to several other counties in Kentucky.

Corn, wheat, tobacco, and soybeans are some of the crops the Kentucky Amish grow to sell, along with various vegetables and flowering plants. Dairy farming is also a popular livelihood, and many Amish people have home-based businesses, selling various products to their English and Amish neighbors.

The Old Order Amish living in Christian County don't use electricity, and their main mode of transportation is horse and buggy. They also hire English drivers to take them places they are not able to go by horse and buggy. Since most of the Amish came from Lancaster County, they continue to drive the gray box-shaped buggies they drove in Pennsylvania. Their style of clothing is the same as in Lancaster County, as well.

The Fairview Produce Auction, not far from Hopkinsville, Kentucky, is well attended by the Christian County Amish, who go there to buy or sell their home-grown produce. Pots of colorful mums are for sale during the fall, and so are pumpkins, squashes, and gourds. The Amish and Mennonites in Kentucky are experienced growers and produce quality products. Some buyers come from as far as Nashville, Cincinnati, and Chicago to obtain Amish-grown produce and products.

Miscellaneous

But let patience have her perfect work,
that ye may be perfect and entire, wanting nothing.

JAMES 1:4

Stove Cleaner

In the evening, put grates or stove parts that need major cleaning in large garbage bag and pour 2 cups ammonia into bag and close tightly. Let set until morning. Parts will be easy to wash. Do not inhale ammonia!

Kate Bontrager
Middlebury, Indiana

Solution for Washing Women's Head Coverings

1 ounce liquid Clorox 2
1 ounce liquid Cascade detergent
1 ounce liquid Wisk or some kind of bluing

Place soaps in 1½-gallon pail and add water. Put as many as 3 coverings in water and soak for a few hours. Rinse with clear water.

Marilyn Hostetler
Topeka, Indiana

Laundry Presoak Spray

1 cup water
1 cup liquid Wisk
1 cup ammonia

Pour all ingredients into spray bottle. Spray liberally on soiled areas of clothing. Let saturate, then scrub and toss into washer. This works for bacon grease, etc.

Mary Miller
Shipshewana, Indiana

Laundry Soap

Fill 5 (1 gallon) pails half full of water (rainwater works best)

Add:

12 ounces lye

7 cups grease, melted

    (½ tallow and ½ lard works well)

1 cup ammonia

2 cups borax

3 cups Wisk or any desired detergent

Mix lye, grease, ammonia, borax, and detergent. Divide evenly into five (1 gallon) pails of water and stir well. Finish filling the gallon pails with water. Several times a day, stir for a few minutes. Do this for 6 or 7 days. Then cover and store until ready to use.

Mrs. Chris Hostetler
Norwalk, Wisconsin

Remedy for Swimmer's Ear

Combine equal parts of rubbing alcohol and white vinegar in a small bottle. Put 2 or 3 drops in ears before and after swimming. The alcohol dries out the ear, and the vinegar acts as an antibacterial agent. A slight pull on the earlobe will be painful to someone who has swimmer's ear.

Prevention hint: After being underwater, tip your head to the side to clear water out of the ears.

Emma Fisher
Ronks, Pennsylvania

Earache Remedy

Mix 2 tablespoons of olive oil and 2 fresh minced garlic buds. Let set a day or two. Strain and use as eardrops for earaches.

Kate Bontrager
Middlebury, Indiana

Chest Congestion
or Cold

Put cider vinegar on a cloth. Place cloth on chest for 2 hours.

Marilyn Hostetler
Topeka, Indiana

Cough Syrup

½ cup cider vinegar
½ cup water
1 teaspoon cayenne pepper
3 tablespoons honey

Mix all ingredients well. Administer by teaspoonfuls. This is also good for sore throats.

Mary and Katie Yoder
Goshen, Indiana

If you insist on perfection, make the demands on yourself.

Fly Spray

3 cups water

2 cups white vinegar

1 cup Avon Skin-So-Soft bath oil

1 tablespoon eucalyptus oil

Put all ingredients in jar and shake. Use as wipe or spray. Lasts 2 to 3 days and keeps flies and mosquitoes away!

Esta Miller
Millersburg, Ohio

Air Freshener

Cut an orange in half. Remove pulp and fill peel with salt. It will provide a pleasant aromatic scent anywhere in your home. Salt also deodorizes thermos bottles and jugs.

To get rid of musty basement smells, put charcoal in flat 1x2-foot box and sprinkle with 1 pint Epsom salt. Scattering a few charcoals here and there also works.

Mattie Stoltzfus
Paradise, Pennsylvania

🌿 Lincoln County, Montana

In 1975 an Amish settlement in northwestern Montana, not far from the Canadian border, had its beginning. Diminishing farmland and overpopulation are part of the reason Amish people have been drawn to Lincoln County, Montana, near the small town of Rexford. Some simply enjoy living near the wooded, mountainous area.

Many of the Amish living in this area, also known as West Kootenai, have log homes. Even the one-room schoolhouse there is made of logs. Many of the Amish make log homes and log furniture. Others raise beef cattle or grow alfalfa hay. Some also operate home-based businesses for a living.

Some horses and buggies are used among the Amish in this area, but most Amish people living in the Rexford community get around on bicycles. When they have to go any distance, they hire an English driver.

Every year on the second Saturday of June, the Rexford Amish host a community auction that brings in over a thousand people—English, Amish, and Mennonite—from far and wide. The items offered up for bid at the auction include such things as farming machinery, hand-stitched quilts, wall hangings, wood carvings, various handcrafted items, log and cedar furniture, gazebos, and even log homes. A portion of the proceeds from the sale of these items goes to the local Amish schoolhouse. The women of the Rexford Amish community serve lunch, featuring barbecued chicken and side dishes. Pies and other baked goods are offered at modest prices. A trip to this event is well worth the drive!

Pickles and Relish

Blessed are the peacemakers:
for they shall be called the children of God.

MATTHEW 5:9

Hamburger Pickles

1 gallon cucumbers, sliced
1 gallon water
1 cup salt
1 tablespoon alum

Put sliced cucumbers in salt brine made of 1 gallon water and 1 cup salt. Let stand 3 days. Drain off. Wash in clear water. Put cucumbers in kettle of water (enough to cover) and add 1 tablespoon alum. Boil 10 minutes. Drain off liquid.

Syrup:
1 pint vinegar
1 pint water
3 pounds sugar
1 tablespoon allspice
1 tablespoon celery seed

Heat syrup ingredients (spice may be put in small cloth bag) and pour over cucumbers. Cook until clear and glossy. Remove spice bag. Put in jars and seal.

Mrs. Miller
Morley, Michigan

Cinnamon Pickles

2 gallons large cucumbers peeled, seeded,
and sliced (about 15 large cucumbers)
2 cups lime juice
8½ cups water

Combine lime juice and 8½ cups water. Pour over cucumbers. Soak 24 hours. Drain and wash cucumbers in cold water 2 times. Cover with cold water and let stand 3 hours. Drain.

Brine:
1 cup vinegar
1 tablespoon alum
1 small bottle red food coloring

Combine vinegar, alum, and food coloring with enough cold water to cover cucumbers. Simmer (not boil) 2 hours. Drain.

Syrup:
3 cups vinegar
11 cups sugar
3 cups water
1 pound cinnamon red hots
10 small cinnamon sticks

Combine vinegar, sugar, water, red hots, and cinnamon sticks. Bring to a boil. Pour syrup over cucumbers. Let stand 24 hours. Drain and reheat syrup. Pour over cucumbers again. Let stand 24 hours. Do this 3 times. Spoon pickles into pint jars. Heat syrup and remove the cinnamon sticks. Pour over pickles in jars. Seal jars and process in boiling water bath 5 minutes. Makes 9 pints.

Rebecca Troyer
Berne, Indiana

7-Day
Sweet Pickles

Wash cucumbers and slice into kettle. For 1 gallon of cucumbers add ¾ cup salt to 1 gallon boiling water. Place plate on top of cucumbers to hold slices underwater. Let stand 4 or 5 days. Drain. Rinse cucumbers. Cover with boiling water and 1½ tablespoons alum and let set for 1 day. Drain. Cover with plain boiling water and let set for 1 day. Drain and rinse.

Syrup:
¾ quart clear vinegar
1 quart water
2 cinnamon sticks
10 cups sugar
1 tablespoon celery seeds or 1½ tablespoons
    mixed pickle spice

Heat syrup. Add pickles and heat slowly to simmering point. Put in hot jars and cap to seal.

Susie J. Miller
Heuvelton, New York

> ◆ ◆ ◆
>
> *Prayer is not a way*
> *of getting what we want,*
> *but the way to become*
> *what God wants us to be.*
>
> ◆ ◆ ◆

Summer Squash Relish

5 pounds yellow summer squash
4 large onions
4 large green peppers, seeded
4 sweet red peppers, seeded
5 tablespoons pickling salt

Grind squash, onions, and peppers into bowl. Add pickling salt. Let stand overnight. Drain and rinse well twice.

In stainless steel kettle, combine the following:

5 cups sugar
3½ cups 5 percent vinegar
2½ teaspoons celery salt
1½ teaspoons ground turmeric
2 teaspoons pickling spice wrapped in cloth

Bring to a boil and boil 5 minutes. Remove spice cloth. Add drained veggies to vinegar mix and bring to a boil. Put into jars and seal. Put jars in water bath and boil 15 minutes. Remove jars and cool on wire racks. Yield: 7 pints

Beverly Stauffer
Elkhorn, Kentucky

> *A mother's patience is like*
> *a tube of toothpaste:*
> *you can always squeeze out*
> *a little bit more.*

Mom's Cucumber Relish

1 peck (2 gallons) cucumbers

6 large onions

⅓ cup salt

3 cups sugar

1 tablespoon celery seed

2 tablespoons mustard seed

½ tablespoon turmeric

2 cups vinegar

Pare and grind cucumbers and onions. Sprinkle salt over mixture and let stand 1 hour. Drain. Combine sugar, spices, and vinegar and pour over vegetables. Cook 5 minutes. Pour into jars and seal.

Elva Shirk
Dundee, New York

🌿Sarasota County, Florida

The Amish community in Sarasota County, Florida, is different than any other Amish community in America. Many Amish and Mennonite people come from their homes around the country to Sarasota during the winter months to enjoy the warm weather and white, sandy beaches. Individuals and families who come for vacation usually rent a place to stay, but some Amish who have retired in the Sarasota neighborhood known as Pinecraft, have purchased small houses or mobile homes as their permanent residence.

The Plain People who come to Pinecraft are from many different states, so a variety of styles in clothing and women's head coverings can be seen there.

There are no horses and buggies in Sarasota for the Amish to drive. Instead, they get around on bicycles and large-wheel tricycles that have a box on the back for transporting their shopping items. The Amish also use public transportation when traveling farther than where it is practical to go on their bikes.

A small farmer's market in the Pinecraft neighborhood is open on Saturdays. During the week, various food items, including oranges and grapefruit, can be purchased from roadside stands in front of Amish homes.

Since the houses are too small for church services to be held in the traditional Amish way, the Amish who live in or visit Sarasota often attend the Mennonite Tourist Church.

Several restaurants in the area serve traditional Pennsylvania Dutch food, and the Amish and other Plain People can often be found eating out. The Amish also enjoy walking on the beach, going deep-sea fishing, or playing golf, shuffleboard, and volleyball. They join thousands of others who trade cold sleet and snow during the winter months for warm sunshine and sandy beaches.

Salads and Sides

Better is little with the fear of the LORD than
great treasure and trouble therewith.

PROVERBS 15:16

Delicious Macaroni Salad

6 cups macaroni, cooked
4 eggs, boiled and chopped
2 cups celery, chopped
2 small onions, chopped
2 cups carrots, shredded

Dressing:
2 cups granulated sugar
½ cup vinegar
½ cup water
1 tablespoon mustard
1 tablespoon butter
4 eggs, beaten
1⅓ cups mayonnaise

Combine macaroni, eggs, celery, onions, and carrots in bowl. In saucepan, combine sugar, vinegar, water, mustard, butter, and eggs. Boil 2 minutes. Cool. Add mayonnaise. If dressing is too thick when cold, add a little cream to it. Stir dressing into salad ingredients until mixed.

Wilma Leinbach
Shippensburg, Pennsylvania

Potato Salad

12 cups potatoes, cooked

12 eggs, boiled

2 cups celery, chopped

1½ cups onion, chopped

3 cups salad dressing

3 tablespoons vinegar

3 tablespoons mustard

4 teaspoons salt

1½ cups sugar

½ cup milk

Cook potatoes and eggs then shred them. Add celery and onion. In separate bowl, mix salad dressing, vinegar, mustard, salt, sugar, and milk. Pour over potato mixture and mix. Best when mixed the day before or several hours before serving.

Mrs. David Graber
Bloomfield, Iowa

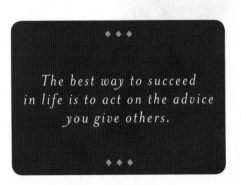

The best way to succeed in life is to act on the advice you give others.

Cabbage Salad

4 quarts cabbage, shredded
1 pepper, finely chopped
2 medium onions, finely chopped

Combine cabbage, pepper, and onions.

Dressing:
1½ cups white sugar
¾ cup vinegar
1 tablespoon salt
¾ cup vegetable oil
1 teaspoon celery salt

Bring sugar, vinegar, salt, oil, and celery salt to a boil. Pour over cabbage mixture and mix well.

Mary Hilty
Berne, Indiana

Grape Salad

1 (8 ounce) package cream cheese, softened
3 to 4 pounds grapes
8 ounces sour cream
1½ cups powdered sugar
8 ounces frozen whipped topping, thawed
1 teaspoon lemon juice

Mix cream cheese and sour cream. Add powdered sugar, whipped topping, and lemon juice. Fold in grapes.

Leah Schwartz
Portland, Indiana

Dreamsicle Salad

1 small box flavored gelatin
¼ cup sugar
1 cup boiling water
½ cup cold water
4 ounces cream cheese
1 (16 ounce) container frozen whipped topping, thawed

Dissolve gelatin and sugar in boiling water. Add cold water. Set in refrigerator until partially congealed. Whip cream cheese well and gradually add whipped topping. Add gelatin and mix well. Refrigerate.

Lila Yoder
Montezuma, GA

Success in marriage is not
finding the right person,
but becoming the
right person.

Spinach Salad

2 pounds fresh spinach
1 medium onion, finely chopped
4 eggs, hard boiled and diced
6 slices bacon, fried and crumbled
½ pound mushrooms, fresh and sliced

Combine all ingredients. Serve with your favorite dressing.

Lovina Petersheim
Osseo, Michigan

Friend Salad

1 head lettuce, torn in small pieces
3 slices Swiss cheese, torn in pieces
1 (10 ounce) box peas, frozen
1 large onion, chopped
2 tablespoons sugar
5 tablespoons mayonnaise
½ pound bacon, fried and crumbled
2 eggs, hard boiled and sliced or chopped

Two or three hours before serving, tear lettuce into small pieces and layer in large serving bowl. Tear Swiss cheese over lettuce. Layer peas and onion. Sprinkle sugar over all then spread with mayonnaise. Cover and let stand in refrigerator 2 to 3 hours. Before serving, top with crumbled bacon and chopped egg. Toss and serve.

Laura Byler
Woodhull, New York

Christmas Salad

2 small boxes strawberry gelatin
1 (20 ounce) can crushed pineapple (reserve juice)
½ cup pecans, chopped
1 package unflavored gelatin dissolved in ¼ cup cold water
1 (8 ounce) package cream cheese, softened
1 cup whipping cream
Sugar and vanilla to taste
2 small boxes lime gelatin

Mix strawberry gelatin with water according to package directions and pour into 9x13-inch cake pan. Let cool in refrigerator to jelly stage. Drain pineapple and save juice. Put half of the pineapple and half of the nuts in red gelatin and let set. Bring pineapple juice to a boil and add unflavored gelatin that has been dissolved in ¼ cup cold water. Add cream cheese to gelatin and let cool until partially set. Whip whipping cream until stiff. Add sugar and vanilla then add to juice and gelatin mixture. Pour on top of red gelatin. Let set. Fix lime gelatin as you did the red, and when it is thickened, put on top of juice and cream mixture and let set until hard. Cut to serve.

Alice Beechy
Pittsford, Michigan

Cranberry Salad

1 small box cherry gelatin
1¼ cups boiling water
1 cup cranberries, ground
1 cup sugar
Water, enough to cook cranberries and sugar in
3 cups apples, ground
1 cup pineapple, crushed

Dissolve gelatin in boiling water and set aside. In large saucepan combine cranberries, sugar, and water and cook until berries are soft. When cool combine with gelatin mixture. Add apples and pineapple. Chill well before serving.

Lydia Hoover
Denver, Pennsylvania

◆ ◆ ◆

The difference between truth and tale is the difference between the photograph in the seed catalog and what comes up in the gardens.

◆ ◆ ◆

Cauliflower Salad

1 head cauliflower, separated into florets
1 head lettuce, torn into bite-size pieces
9 slices bacon, cooked and crumbled
1 large sweet onion, sliced and separated into rings
1 cup Parmesan cheese, grated

Dressing:
1¾ cups mayonnaise
⅓ cup sugar

In large salad bowl, layer the cauliflower, lettuce, bacon, onion, and cheese. Cover and chill several hours. Prepare dressing. When ready to serve, pour dressing over salad and toss. Yield: 8 to 10 servings

Mary Newswanger
Shippensburg, Pennsylvania

Mom's Bean Salad

1 (15 ounce) can green beans, drained
1 (15 ounce) can yellow beans, drained
1 (15 ounce) can kidney beans, drained
1 (10 ounce) box frozen lima beans
1 cup carrots, cooked
1 large onion, sliced thin
1 green mango, cut in strips
3 stalks celery, cut in chunks

Mix above ingredients.

Dressing:
2 cups white sugar
½ cup water
1½ cups vinegar
½ cup salad oil
1 teaspoon celery seed
1 teaspoon salt

Mix dressing ingredients and wait until sugar is dissolved. Pour over drained bean mix. Let stand 24 hours before serving.

Susan Miller
Millersburg, Ohio

Good Pink Stuff

⅔ cup cherry gelatin
2 pints hot water
2 cups miniature marshmallows
1 cup whipped cream
1 (8 ounce) package cream cheese, softened

Dissolve gelatin in hot water. Add marshmallows. Chill. When cool add whipped cream and cream cheese.

Mrs. Jonas S. Gingerich
Dalton, Ohio

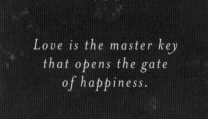

*Love is the master key
that opens the gate
of happiness.*

Fruit Salad

1 (8 ounce) package cream cheese, softened
1 (14 ounce) can sweetened condensed milk
¼ cup lemon juice
1 (16 ounce) container frozen whipped topping, thawed
2 cups seedless grapes
4 apples, cut up
2 oranges, cut up
3 bananas, cut up
2 cups pineapple chunks

Mix cream cheese, condensed milk, and lemon juice. Fold in whipped topping and add fresh fruit.

Maria Schrock
Princeton, Missouri

Melon Summer Salad

1 cup watermelon balls
1 cup cantaloupe or honeydew melon balls
Juice of 1 lemon
¼ cup honey
½ cup whipping cream, whipped stiff
Lettuce leaves for serving

Sprinkle fruit balls with lemon juice then drizzle with honey. Chill. Just before serving, fold in whipped cream. Serve on crisp lettuce.

Mrs. Joe J. Miller
Lakeview, Michigan

*Some small deed
may help to brighten
someone else's day.*

Layered Vegetable Salad

1 head lettuce
1 medium onion, sliced
½ cup green pepper, sliced
1 cup celery, diced
1 cup cauliflower florets
1 cup broccoli florets
1½ cups green peas, frozen
½ to 1 pound bacon, fried crisp and broken in pieces
4 eggs, hard boiled and sliced

Tear lettuce into bite-size pieces and layer in large bowl. Layer remaining vegetables and bacon. Layer eggs on top.

Dressing:
1 cup mayonnaise
1 cup sour cream
2 tablespoons white sugar
4 ounces cheddar cheese, grated

Combine mayonnaise, sour cream, and sugar. Spread over top of salad. Refrigerate 4 to 6 hours. Before serving, sprinkle with cheese.

Amanda H. Hershberger
Navarre, Ohio

Cottage Cheese
Garden Salad

4 green onions, finely chopped
6 to 8 radishes, diced
1 green pepper, diced
1 stalk celery, diced
2 carrots, grated
1 tablespoon Miracle Whip
1 (8 ounce) carton cottage cheese
Salt and pepper to taste

Mix all ingredients.

Norma Zimmerman
Latham, Missouri

Hot Chicken Salad

1 cup celery, diced
2 to 3 cups chicken, cooked and chopped
1 can cream of chicken soup
2 to 3 eggs, hard boiled and chopped
1 teaspoon onions, minced
1 cup rice, cooked
¾ cup Miracle Whip
Salt and pepper to taste
1 cup potato chips, crushed

Preheat oven to 350 degrees. Combine celery, chicken, soup, eggs, onions, rice, Miracle Whip, salt, and pepper. Put into greased casserole and cover with crushed potato chips. Bake 25 minutes.

Laura Byler
Woodhull, New York

Yogurt Ranch
Dressing

2½ cups plain yogurt

¾ cup sour cream

¾ cup milk

½ teaspoon dill weed

1½ teaspoons salt

¾ teaspoon garlic powder

2 tablespoons parsley flakes

Combine yogurt, sour cream, milk, dill weed, salt, garlic powder, and parsley flakes. Chill.

Wilma Yoder
Dundee, Ohio

> *Wisdom has two parts:*
> *having much to say and not*
> *saying much at all.*

French Dressing

I cup ketchup
I tablespoon mustard
½ cup sugar
½ cup vinegar
½ cup salad oil
I teaspoon salt

Mix ketchup, mustard, sugar, vinegar, salad oil, and salt. Chill.

Mrs. Levi Schwartz
Geneva, Indiana

Sweet and Sour Sauce

1 cup white sugar

1 cup vegetable oil

1 tablespoon salad dressing

2 tablespoons mustard

1 medium onion, finely diced

¼ cup vinegar

¼ cup water

1 teaspoon salt

1 teaspoon celery seed

¼ teaspoon pepper

Mix all ingredients and chill.

Elsie Mast
Shilo, Ohio

Chicken BBQ Sauce

¼ cup butter

1 cup vinegar

1 cup water

2 ¼ tablespoons salt

1 tablespoon Worcestershire Sauce

Combine all ingredients in saucepan and bring to boil. Brush sauce on chicken while grilling.

L. R. Byler
Atlantic, Pennsylvania

Marinade for Steak or Pork Chops

1½ cups salad oil

¾ cup soy sauce

½ cup wine vinegar

1 teaspoon garlic powder

4 tablespoons Worcestershire sauce

2 tablespoons dry mustard

⅓ cup lemon juice

2 teaspoons salt

2 teaspoons pepper

Combine all ingredients and soak meat in marinade for 1 to 2 days before grilling.

Kate Bontrager
Middlebury, Indiana

Nothing is as strong as gentleness or as gentle as real strength.

Barbecued Green Beans

4 strips bacon, diced
1 onion, finely diced
½ cup sugar
½ cup ketchup
¼ cup vinegar
1 quart green beans

Dice bacon and brown. Drain off part of fat and add onion, sugar, ketch-up, and vinegar. Add beans and simmer 10 to 15 minutes.

Martha Yoder
Crofton, Kentucky

Chili Corn

1 (8 ounce) package cream cheese, softened
4 tablespoons margarine, melted
3 ounce can green chilies, chopped
2 (15 ounce) cans corn, drained

Preheat oven to 350 degrees. Mix all ingredients. Put in casserole and bake 15 to 25 minutes or until bubbly. (Note: 2 (10 ounce) boxes frozen corn may be substituted for canned corn.)

Mrs. Terrence Wenger
Elkhorn, Kentucky

Baked Cabbage

6 cups cabbage
6 tablespoons butter
6 tablespoons flour
1 tablespoon salt
½ teaspoon pepper
3 cups milk
1½ cups cheese, shredded
½ cup bread crumbs

Preheat oven to 350 degrees. Shred cabbage and cook 8 minutes. Drain and put in casserole dish. In saucepan, melt butter and stir in flour and seasonings. Add milk and stir until mixture is combined. Pour over cabbage. Sprinkle cheese and bread crumbs around outer edge of casserole. Bake 20 minutes.

Janet Martin
Ephrata, Pennsylvania

*A flower must go through
a lot of dirt before
it will bloom.*

Zucchini Patties

⅔ cup dry baking mix
¼ cup Parmesan cheese
2 eggs
2 cups zucchini, grated
1 small onion, chopped
Salt and pepper to taste

Combine all ingredients and drop by spoon into heavy skillet covered with oil or butter. Spread out and flatten each patty as you turn it over with a spatula. Fry until golden brown on both sides.

Mrs. Urie Weaver
Bellville, Ohio

Lawrence County, Tennessee

In 1944 three Amish families moved from Mississippi to Lawrence County, Tennessee, looking for a new place to settle. Today about two hundred Amish families live in Lawrence County around the small town of Ethridge. This group of Amish, known as the Swartzentruber Amish, are among some of the most conservative. They live without indoor plumbing, the use of telephones, or any kind of electricity or other modern conveniences.

These very plain Amish live a quiet life with fewer tourists visiting their area than larger Amish communities. They make their living farming crops such as corn, wheat, oats, hay, peanuts, tobacco, and popcorn. They do all their farming with horses and without the aid of modern machinery.

The Lawrence County Amish also sell various homemade products: furniture, baskets, candles, soap, harnesses, braided rugs, and numerous food items. Some also make buggies and shoe horses, own sawmills, and do harness work for a living.

They drive both open and closed black buggies and also use long, open wagons with iron wheels to haul their produce and other large items. A produce auction in the area brings in Amish and English alike.

 # Snacks

And my people shall dwell in a peaceable habitation,
and in sure dwellings, and in quiet resting places.

Isaiah 32:18

Crispy Caramel Corn

2 sticks butter
2 cups brown sugar
½ cup light corn syrup
1 teaspoon salt
½ teaspoon soda
1 teaspoon vanilla
6 to 8 quarts popped corn

Preheat oven to 250 degrees. Melt butter; add sugar, corn syrup, and salt. Boil 5 minutes. Remove from heat and add soda and vanilla. Pour over popcorn and mix well. Bake on greased baking sheets for ½ to 1 hour. Stir every 15 minutes while baking. Let cool.

Mrs. Mahlon Gingerich
Utica, Ohio

Caramel Corn Pops

½ pound butter (not margarine)
1 cup brown sugar
½ cup light corn syrup
1 teaspoon baking soda
Corn Pops (8 ounce package)

Preheat oven to 250 degrees. In 2-quart saucepan, boil butter, sugar, and corn syrup 2 minutes. Add baking soda. Soda will make mixture foam, which is why you need a 2-quart kettle. Pour syrup over Corn Pops and stir until mixed. Pour on greased baking sheet and bake 1 hour, stirring every 15 minutes. Pour on waxed paper and break apart when cool.

Dianna Yoder
Goshen, Indiana

◆ ◆ ◆

Trust is the most valuable thing you will ever earn.

◆ ◆ ◆

Finger Jell-O

4 tablespoons unflavored gelatin
3 (3 ounce) packages any flavor gelatin
4 cups boiling water

In large bowl, combine unflavored and flavored gelatin in boiling water.
Stir until gelatin is dissolved. Pour into large shallow baking pan and refrigerate until firm. Cut into squares to serve.

Verna Wengerd
Walhonding, Ohio

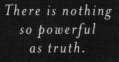

*There is nothing
so powerful
as truth.*

Dip for Fresh Fruit

1 (8 ounce) package cream cheese, softened
1 (7 ounce) jar marshmallow creme

Mix cream cheese and marshmallow creme until light and fluffy. Serve with any kind of fresh fruit.

*Betty Yoder
Rexford, Montana*

Ranch Snack Mix

1 (12 ounce) package pretzels
2 (6 ounce) packages Bugles
1 (10 ounce) can cashews
1 (6 ounce) package bite-size cheddar cheese fish crackers
1 envelope ranch salad dressing mix
¾ cup vegetable oil

In large bowl, combine pretzels, Bugles, cashews, and fish crackers. Sprinkle with dressing mix. Toss gently to combine. Drizzle with oil until well coated. Store in airtight containers.

Edna Mast
Middlebury, Indiana

Sausage Cheese Balls

2 pounds sausage, uncooked
1½ cups dry baking mix
16 ounces (4 cups) cheddar cheese, shredded
½ cup onion, finely chopped
½ cup celery, finely chopped
½ teaspoon garlic powder

Preheat oven to 375 degrees. Mix all ingredients. Form into 1-inch balls.
Bake on ungreased baking sheet 15 minutes or until golden brown. Sausage
balls can be frozen uncooked to be baked later. Yield: approximately
6 dozen

Mrs. Ferlin Yoder
Trenton, Kentucky

Index

SNACKS

Notes

Notes

Notes

Notes

Notes